THE SMALL ISLES

THE SMALL ISLES
Canna, Rum, Eigg and Muck

Denis Rixson

Birlinn

First published in 2001 by Birlinn Limited
8 Canongate Venture
5 New Street
Edinburgh
EH8 8BH

www.birlinn.co.uk

ISBN 1 84158 154 2

British Library Cataloguing-in-Publication Data
A catalogue record for this book is available from the British Library

Typeset by Initial Typesetting Services, Edinburgh
Printed and bound by Omnia Books Limited, Glasgow

Contents

Maps

Figures

Population Tables

Introduction

THIS BOOK OFFERS A history of the Small Isles – Canna, Rum, Eigg and Muck. Like other small islands they have been extensively written about, both individually and collectively. I have no wish to simply repeat what can be found elsewhere. Relevant books and articles are listed in the Bibliography for those who wish to pursue their research. Instead I have picked up common themes, certain traits which help define their economic and cultural history.

Some aspects of island life will always be individual – the local geology and geography, the presence or absence of good soil, harbours and fuel. Such factors determine the particular features of settlement. In more recent times questions such as political and religious affiliation, and above all ownership, have modified island life. But for most of their history these islands shared a common environment, a common climate and a common economic and cultural framework. That is the subject of this book.

For the early history of the islands we have little more than the patchy archaeological record. This reflects the haphazard way in which such research was conducted on the west coast, in turn largely determined by the interests of individual landowners. In the nineteenth century Eigg was owned by Professor Norman Macpherson, a keen antiquarian who excavated a number of sites himself. In recent times Rum and Canna have undergone more thorough investigation. We have a substantial number of Early Christian carvings, some Viking grave-goods, but very little documentary evidence before the sixteenth century. From then on there is an explosion of topographical material; not all of which is truly original since early writers borrowed freely from each other.

Island life changed radically during the nineteenth century as the old economy fell apart. From then on the fortunes of each island depended increasingly upon the family that owned it. It was a fatal dependence, but the fundamental cause was not so much landlord power as the relative economic failure of the Highlands and Islands. Their peripheral economy was too fragile to cope with imperial and industrial Britain.

The old history of the Small Isles as independent economic communities came to an end between about 1750 and 1820. From then on the islands changed hands increasingly often and the people were largely cleared from Rum and Muck. Islanders became subject to the whims and caprices of their owners, their benevolence or otherwise. Much of this recent history has been charted, and repeated, elsewhere, but the economic impasse had been reached by about 1820.

Acknowledgements

I owe a good deal to the staff of Highland Council Library Service. Studying in a remote location is difficult, and they have helped greatly. I should like to thank Norman Newton, Gail Priddice and Edwina Burridge for all their assistance and in particular Sue Skelton and Lorna Skelly for so patiently fulfilling my endless requests. I am also grateful to Mrs Campbell of Canna for her kind hospitality when I was taking photographs of carved stones.

I wish to thank the Scottish Gaelic Texts Society for permission to quote from N. Ross's *Heroic Poetry from the Book of the Dean of Lismore* and Edinburgh University Press for permission to quote from *Iona: The Earliest Poetry of a Celtic Monastery* by Clancy and Markus (copyright Thomas Owen Clancy and Gilbert Markus 1995).

Photographic acknowledgements

I am grateful to the Royal Commission on the Ancient and Historical Monuments of Scotland for permission to publish a number of their photographs. I am also grateful to the Württembergisches Landesmuseum, Stuttgart, Germany, for permission to publish a plate on the stone from Waldenbuch.

Note

Place-names in the Highlands and Hebrides can be spelled in a bewildering number of ways. For ease of identification I have generally followed modern Ordnance Survey spellings. Exceptions occur when I am quoting from a source and wish my accompanying text to match.

When quoting from early accounts I give the date of composition if that is significantly earlier than the date of first publication.

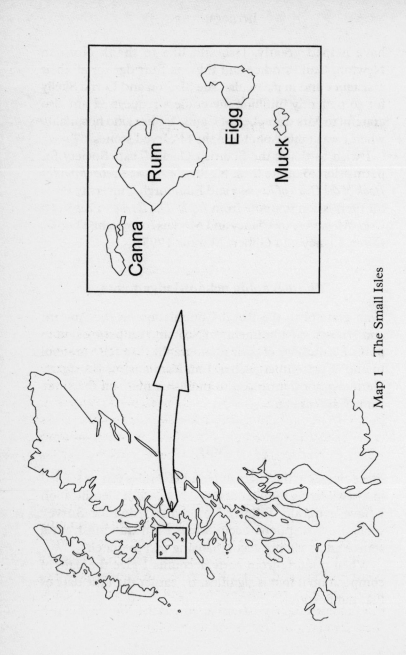

Map 1   The Small Isles

1

Prehistory

Rum

A MESOLITHIC BEACH SITE above the north-west corner
of Loch Scresort provides one of the earliest examples
of human settlement in Scotland. Radiocarbon dates give
an occupation range between about 6500 and 5500 BC.
The site seems to have been used for domestic purposes,
possibly all year round, and stakeholes suggest structures
such as windbreaks or tents. One of the attractions of Rum
was the presence of bloodstone which could be worked
into tools and weapons; while not as good as flint at least
it was available locally on Bloodstone Hill.

These earliest settlers have been described as 'strand-
loopers' or 'hunter-gatherers'. Essentially their economy
was based on collecting whatever food sources occurred
naturally. Only when people came together in larger
communities and started farming, did they have the
numbers and resources to erect large-scale public
monuments such as chambered cairns. We distinguish
these latter groups by the name Neolithic.

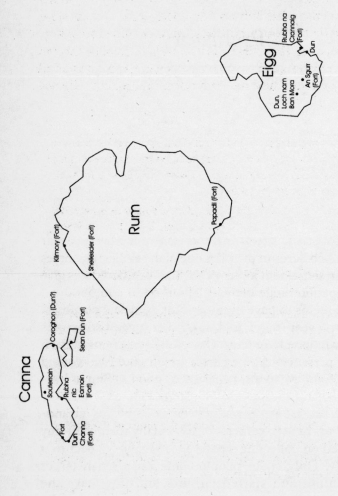

Canna

Souterrain

Coroghon (Dun?)

Rubha
nic
Eamoin
(Fort)

Sean Dun (Fort)

Fort

Dun
Channa
(Fort)

Rum

Kilmoy (Fort)

Shellesder (Fort)

Papadil (Fort)

Eigg

Rubha na
Crannaig
(Fort)

Dun

An Sgurr
(Fort)

Dun,
Loch nam
Ban Mora

Muck

Dun?

Caisteal an Duin Bhain (Fort)

Map 2   Prehistoric sites in the Small Isles

Map 2 shows a number of ancient monuments in the Small Isles. Unfortunately there has been a dearth of proper archaeological excavation and we can say little other than mark their distribution. Moreover, some of these sites, particularly the forts and duns, were occupied for many centuries after their first construction. Defences thrown up in the Iron Age may still have been in use in mediaeval times. Such sites drew comments from the earliest visitors.

Muck

> There is ane Illand called Illand Muck . . . and there is a strenght in it on a rock or craig builded be the Master and Superior of the Illand in tyme of warrs which was betwixt him and certaine enemies.
>
> (Mitchell (ed.) *Macfarlane's Geographical Collections*, vol. II, p. 175, ?1590s)

Eigg

There is a defensive wall on the Sgurr of Eigg and a small dun in the nearby Loch nam Ban Mora.

> And there is ane high mountaine on the southwest syde of this Countrey. And it is ane verie good strength against enemies, that wold doe anie harme or skaith to the Countrey for it wold keep themselves that are Inhabitants of the Iland saiff, and their wyffs and children with all their moveable goods or geir which they could bring or carie with them to the tope of that hill, or mountaine. In this mountaine there is a Mure, and Mosses and in the midst of the tope of that mountaine there is a fresh water Logh. And in the midst of that Logh there is ane Illand which wold hold a certain number of men and women with their bairnes.
>
> (ibid. pp. 175–6)

Crannogs (loch-houses), and island duns sometimes had underwater causeways linking them to the shore.

There is a mountain in the south end, and on the top of it there is a high rock called Skur Egg, about an hundred and fifty paces in circumference, and has a fresh-water lake in the middle of it; there is no access to this rock but by one passage, which makes it a natural fort.

(Martin *A Description of the Western Islands of Scotland*, c. 1695)

The Loch contains an island with remains of mason work, and an under-water footway, which seems to be really a ridge of rock.

(Robertson 'Topography and Traditions of Eigg', 1898)

The Revd F. M'Clymont wrote to Blundell:

There is a funny tradition of its being inhabited by abnormally big women, who used stepping-stones so far apart that none else could use them.

(Blundell *Proceedings of the Scottish Antiquarian Society*, 1913)

The following remarks suggest there may once have been more souterrains or earth-houses:

Eg . . . Thair is mony coves under the earth in this Ile, quhilk the cuntrie folkis uses as strenthis hiding thame and thair geir thairintill;

(Skene *The Description of the Isles of Scotland*, 1577–95)

About thirty yards from the church there is a sepulchral urn under ground; . . . Some few paces to the north of the urn there is a narrow stone passage under ground, but how far it reaches they could give me no account.

(Martin *A Description of the Western Islands of Scotland*, c. 1695)

Canna

In this Ile is ane heich craig callit Corignan weill braid on the heicht thairof, and but ane strait passage, that men may scairslie climb to the heid of the craig, and quhan the cuntrie is invadit the people gadderis thair wives and geir to the heid of the craig and defend thame selfis utherwayis the best thay may, and will not pass to the craig, because it may not be lang keepit onlie for fault of water.

[In this isle there is a high crag called Coroghon which is broad on the summit and with only one narrow access. When the island is invaded the men put their wives and goods into the Coroghon whilst they defend themselves as best they can. They will not go to the Coroghon themselves because it cannot be defended for long since it lacks water.]

(Skene The Description of the Isles of Scotland, 1577–95)

Visit a lofty slender rock, that juts into the sea: on one side is a little tower, at a vast height above us, accessible by a narrow and horrible path: it seems so small as scarce to be able to contain half a dozen people. Tradition says, that it was built by some jealous regulus, to confine a handsome wife in.

(Pennant A Tour in Scotland and Voyage to the Hebrides, 1772)

Bloodstone

Bloodstone was an important natural resource in Stone Age Rum. Flint was not available locally but bloodstone provided an alternative for making tools and weapons. Finds of bloodstone on other sites suggest it was valued and traded as a commodity. Even in the nineteenth century men came for bloodstone, at some risk in the stormy seas.

The expedition to Rum ended as many others had done before. I had ballasted the boat with as much bloodstone as would have furnished all the shops in London. But still it blew hard, the boat would not scud, and I was obliged to throw the ballast overboard. Gold and silver have gone the same road too often, to justify any especial lamentation over half a ton of jasper. There was a blockhead on board who thought fit to cry, because, as he said, he had a wife and children, and did not choose to risk his life for a 'wheen chucky-stanes'.

(MacCulloch *The Highlands and Western Isles of Scotland*, vol. IV, 1824)

Hunting and gathering

A recurrent theme today is the notion that somehow we have to rediscover a past ability to live in harmony with our environment. Primitive peoples apparently have this, and in our capitalist world we have forgotten it. We exploit, but do not sustain; we exhaust, but do not enrich – the soil, the sea, the air. The Hebrides are a good environment in which to explore this issue. Did we destroy this Garden of Eden? Or did it collapse from within?

The first settlers in the Small Isles practised a hunter-gatherer economy. This was the case throughout the Hebrides. Shellfish offer the only assured, year-round food supply; so people camped on the beach. They ate shellfish, in their millions, and gathered nuts, berries and edible plants as the seasons offered. Some early shell-middens are so enormous that these first communities may have exhausted the supplies on particular beaches and had to move on in search of new resources. (There is a large shell-midden at Papadil, Rum). No doubt these early groups also pursued animals, set traps for game and snares for birds.

The economy of the West Highlands and Islands has retained this hunter-gatherer element throughout its history. The scant resources of the region meant that people have always been constrained to hunt and gather as opportunity offered. There was seldom a sufficient surplus to allow them to forego this. So shellfish remained a staple even in the eighteenth century, despite the success of the potato and the area's recently enforced contact with the outside world. In Skye:

> The poor are left to Providence's care: they prowl like other animals along the shores to pick up limpets and other shell-fish, the casual repasts of hundreds during part of the year in these unhappy islands. Hundreds thus annually drag through the season a wretched life.
>
> (Pennant *A Tour in Scotland and Voyage to the Hebrides*, 1772)

It was the same in north-east Scotland:

> For it is well known, that from the month of March, to the middle of August, some poor upon the coast, have nothing but shell-fish, such as muscles [sic], cockles, and the like, to support them.
>
> (*Life of Barisdale*, 1754)

Of course larger game were also pursued. Animals such as seals, otters, deer, salmon, geese, seabirds, all yielded valuable products: skin, oil, fur, food and feathers. We are most familiar with this aspect of the Highland economy in the context of St Kilda, where the culling of seabirds was most developed and lasted longest. However it was formerly widespread, from Ailsa Craig to North Rona, both places which were reckoned of value for their seabird harvests. Seals were culled regularly. The slaughter of 'selchis' features prominently in the accounts of Dean Monro and Martin Martin.

The Small Isles offer numerous examples of a marginal economy which perpetually has to fall back on its scant resources and its hunter-gatherer techniques. Here follow some extracts about the natural resources that could be gathered, harvested or culled.

Tidal fish-traps

In Rum there were tidal fish-traps at Kinloch and, apparently, Kilmory. These are common throughout the Highlands and Islands although many of them, because they lie below the water-line, are now unnoticed or forgotten. Sometimes a place-name including the Gaelic word *caraidh* (or *cairidh*) gives us a clue. Unfortunately these traps are undated and probably for the most part undateable.

On the map there is still a Camas na Cairidh in Muck. There had, according to information given to the School of Scottish Studies in 1976, formerly been a *caraidh* in Canna and another in Sanday. Walls were built below the tide line, the fish came in with the tide and were trapped by the walls when the tide went out. Although these were doubtless reused and rebuilt many times over the centuries they are probably very ancient.

At Raonapoll, Rum:

> The pool is fed by the streamlet which wanders down the mountain side through the little ravine. When the tide is out the pool is not more than twenty yards across; and it empties itself into the sea by a short channel about two yards in width. When the tide is in, however, the influx of water from the bay increases the pool very considerably, and, at the same time, brings into it fish from the sea, which are easily caught by netting in the narrow channel, before the water retires.

(Waugh *The Limping Pilgrim*, 1882)

8

Shellfish and migratory fish
(Salmon and Sea-trout)

Shellfish continued to be a critically important food source for people in the Small Isles until quite recently. In 1794 Donald M'Lean, the minister, wrote of the predicament of:

> a married common labourer in husbandry ... Many of them have one fourth of the crop they make with the plough, being generally barley and oats, and a third of the crop they make with the spade, and manure with sea-ware, which is principally potatoes, and grazing for two cows with their followers. This must afford them but a scanty subsistence, especially in years of scarcity, when they have a numerous family of weak children; but, with the aid derived from the shore, they are enabled to live.

Continual pressure on shellfish as a food source probably took its toll, especially on those beaches closest to populated areas such as Cleadale. It is possible that a beach once rich in shellfish was simply cleaned out. We may have a rationalisation of this in a story about

> The traditional ploughing of Laig beach, by which one of the richest beaches in shell-fish in the Hebrides was rendered utterly barren.

> (Robertson 'Topography and
> Traditions of Eigg', 1898)

This vengeful act is associated with the Macleod raid in the sixteenth century which led up to the massacre in Uamh Fhraing. However there is a similar tradition in connection with a beach at Barrisdale in Knoydart which was supposedly ploughed up by Hanoverians after the 1745 Rising. It seems more likely that in both these cases the beaches became exhausted by human pressure and that a convenient scapegoat was sought.

Rum

The rivers on each side afford salmon.

(Martin *A Description of the Western Islands of Scotland, c.* 1695)

There was light enough left, as we reached the upper part of Loch Scresort, to show us a shoal of small silver-coated trout, leaping by scores at the effluence of the little stream . . . There was a net stretched across where the play was thickest; and we learned that the haul of the previous tide had amounted to several hundreds. On reaching the *Betsey*, we found a pail and basket laid against the companion-head – the basket containing about two dozen small trout – the minister's unsolicited teind of the morning draught; the pail filled with razor-fish of great size. . . . The razor-fish had been brought us by the worthy catechist of the island. He had gone to the ebb in our special behalf, and had spent a tide in laboriously filling the pail with these 'treasures hid in the sand' . . .

We were told . . . that the expatriated inhabitants of Rum used to catch trout by a simple device of ancient standing, which preceded the introduction of nets into the island, and which, it is possible, may in other localities have not only preceded the use of the net, but may have also suggested it: it had at least the appearance of being a first beginning of invention in this direction. The islanders gathered large quantities of heath, and then tying it loosely into bundles, and stripping it of its softer leafage, they laid the bundles across the stream on a little mound held down by stones, with the tops of the heath turned upwards to the current. The water rose against the mound for a foot or eighteen inches, and then murmured over and through, occasioning an expansion among the hard elastic sprays. Next a party of the islanders came down the stream, beating the banks and pools, and sending a still thickening shoal of trout before them, that, on reaching the miniature dam formed by the bundles, darted forward for shelter, as if to a hollow bank, and stuck among the slim hard branches, as they would in the meshes of a net. The stones were then hastily thrown off, – the bundles pitched ashore, – the better fish, to the amount not unfrequently of several scores, secured, – and the young fry returned to the stream, to take care of themselves, and grow bigger. We fared richly this evening, after our hard day's labour, on tea and trout.

(Miller *The Cruise of the Betsey*, 1845)

Seabirds and their eggs

Seabirds were a very important economic resource throughout the Hebrides. This is one reason why they feature so often in early topographical accounts. They were important for food, feathers and fat. Even today their eggs are occasionally used. In the following accounts solan geese are gannets, puffins are Manx Shearwaters and penguins are probably puffins!

RONIN.[RUM] . . . In this ile will be gotten about Britane als many wild nests upon the plane mure as men pleasis to gadder, and yet by resson the fowls hes few to start them except deir. . . . Maney solan geise are in this ile. . . .

EGGA. . . . many solan geese.

(Monro *A Description of the Western Isles of Scotland*, 1549)

J. L. Campbell thought Britane was a mistake for Beltane, that is, 1 May. An unknown author, probably Timothy Pont, writes of the Manx shearwaters in Rum and Canna in the 1590s. He had obviously eaten them and found them oily.

And certane foullis which will be taken in these mountaines and are exceeding fatt, of the fattest birds or foulis which is in all the sea they are no bigger then a dove or somewhat les in bignes. Somewhat gray in coloure of their feathers being of the most delicate birds to be eaten that is bred within the whole Illand, except that doe taste oyld. . . .

Cainna . . . And there is verie manie of these foulls and birds aforsaid which are found in Rhum, are found in this Illand.

(Mitchell (ed.) *Macfarlane's Geographical Collections*, vol. II, p. 177, ?1590s)

Rum . . . hath certaine wild fowles about the bigness of a dow, gray coloured, which ar scarce in uthir places, good meat they ar.

(ibid. p. 528)

Then Ruma . . . the sea fowles lay their egges heere and there in the ground. In the middest of spring time, when the egges are laid, any man may take of them. In the high rockes, the solayne geese are taken in abundance. . . . In Egga are solayne geese.

(*A Short Description of the Western Isles of Scotland*, printed in *Miscellanea Scotica*, 1818)

The advantage of Manx Shearwaters was that they nested in burrows high in the cliffs and hills. Here they could be caught easily.

RUM . . . There is plenty of land and sea-fowl; some of the latter, especially the puffin, build in the hills as much as in the rocks on the coast, in which there are abundance of caves

(Martin *A Description of the Western Islands of Scotland, c.* 1695)

Rum . . . in all parts, there is great Abundance of Moorfool.

. . . The Puffin of the Isle of Man also builds here, which is reckoned the greatest Delicacy of all Sea Birds. It is rarely to be met with in other places, and keeps the Sea all the year round except in hatching Time. It builds in Holes under Ground, and we found its Nests among the loose Rocks, above a Mile from the Shore.

(Walker *Report on the Hebrides*, 1764)

The puffins are found in considerable numbers, which, though sea fowls, lay and hatch sometimes at a great distance from the shore, even near the tops of high hills. Their young, before they leave the nest, are as large as the dam, transparent with fat, and delicious to the taste of many.

(M'Lean *Old Statistical Account, Parish of Small Isles*, 1794)

The puffin, a comparatively rare bird in the inner Hebrides, builds, I was told, in great numbers in the continuous line of precipice which, after sweeping for a full mile round the Bay of Laig, forms the pinnacled rampart here, and then, turning another angle of the island, runs on parallel to the coast for about six miles more. In former times the puffin furnished the islanders, as in St Kilda, with a staple article of food, in those hungry months of summer in which the stores of the old crop had begun to fail, and the new crop had not yet ripened; . . . I found among the islanders what was said to be a piece of the natural history of the puffin, sufficiently apocryphal . . . The puffin feeds its young, say the islanders, on an oily scum of the sea, which renders it such an unwieldy mass of fat, that about the time when it should be beginning to fly, it becomes unable to get out of its hole. The parent bird, not in the least puzzled, however, treats the case medicinally, and, – like mothers of another two-legged genus, who, when their daughters get over-stout, put them through a course of reducing acids to bring them down, – feeds it on sorrel-leaves for several days together, till, like a boxer under

13

training, it gets thinned to the proper weight, and becomes able not only to get out of its cell, but also to employ its wings.

(Miller *The Cruise of the Betsey,* 1845)

One early traveller, L. A. Necker de Saussure, found the change from Switzerland to the Hebrides rather overwhelming. The waters may have appeared icy but for one type of seabird he was badly served by his eyesight or his imagination.

We had near us, on the west, the high and wild mountains of the Isle of Rum; on the north, the fine mountains of the Isle of Sky, with their tops covered with snow. The sea rolled its high billows, and broke against the rocks; whilst innumerable flights of sea-gulls, penguins, and other birds inhabiting the icy seas, were swimming, plunging, and flying.

(Necker de Saussure
A Voyage to the Hebrides, 1807)

Geese

ISLE CANNAY

. . . the rock Heisker on the south end abounds with wild geese in August, and then they cast their quills.

(Martin *A Description of the Western Islands of Scotland, c.* 1695)

Whales, seals, otters

Sail under the vast mountains of Rum, and the point of Bredon, through a most turbulent sea, caused by the clashing of two adverse tides. See several small whales, called here Pollacks, that when near land are often chaced on shore by boats: they are usually about ten feet long, and yield four gallons of oil.

> (Pennant *A Tour in Scotland and Voyage to the Hebrides*, 1772)

Of the otter:

As he preys in the sea, he does little visible mischief, and is killed only for his fur.

> (Johnson *A Journey to the Western Islands of Scotland*, 1773)

The amphibious animals are seals and otters; the blubber of the one is made into oil, and the skin of the other is sold for fur, at a price proportionate to its size; some of them have been sold for above 12s. Sterling.

> (M'Lean *Old Statistical Account, Parish of Small Isles*, 1794)

For comparison a female domestic servant received annually from 12s. to 20s. (with shoes etc.) and the price of a sheep was about 4s.

Beach wreck and driftwood

Of Guirdil, Rum:

We landed near a farm, called Guidhl . . . where we were regaled with new milk, oat-cakes, and Lisbon wine. I was surprised to find wine of that species, and of a superior quality in such a hut, but they told us it was part of the freight of some unfortunate vessel wrecked near the island, whose cargo came on shore.

> (Edward Daniel Clarke, 1797)

I observed for the first time in the interior of this cottage, what I had frequent occasion to remark afterwards, that

15

much of the wood used in buildings in the smaller and outer islands of the Hebrides must have drifted across the Atlantic, borne eastwards and northwards by the great gulf-stream. Many of the beams and boards . . . are of American timber, that from time to time has been cast upon the shore.

(Miller *The Cruise of the Betsey,* 1845)

Poverty, and the absence of proper resources meant that islanders had to manage as they could. This 'mend and make do' approach had its down side, as Waugh illustrates in a story about a 'new' bridge in Rum which replaced one carried away by the great tide of November 1881.

The three planks which made the footpath of the former bridge were carried away; and the only one of the three which was recovered was the cracked plank, which had been incorporated with the new bridge. This plank, with the addition of a deal baulk, – part of the wreck of some timber-laden ship, – now form the sole footpath of the new bridge; and for one foot that treads upon the plank, there are twenty that choose the deal baulk. A simple wooden rail on one side only, completes the bridge, which is less than two feet wide, including the cracked plank. . . . The other day, when the stream was swollen with heavy rain, old Mackinnon, the gardener, was trying to wheel a barrowful of dirty clothes across the bridge; and not daring to trust the wheel upon the cracked plank, he was compelled to tilt his barrow so much on one side, that, at last, he overbalanced it, and down it went into the stream, with him after it. The fall was only about six feet; but it was quite enough at once, for an old man. He was crooning Gaelic verse when he came across the meadow; but, as he clambered up the bank out of that stream, he was talking prose.

Edwin Waugh goes on to describe how virtually everything was made from driftwood:

There are no timber yards, nor joiners' shops, upon this island; and, with the exception of a few nails, which fasten the patch upon the cracked plank, the little bridge is entirely made out of wreck-wood brought ashore by the waves; indeed, nearly all kinds of simple household woodwork, such as tables, chairs, shelves, and chests for the living, and coffins for the dead, – such as the rude box in which the remains of 'the old captain' were lately laid in the old graveyard at Kilmory, – are made of these waifs of wreck from the wild ocean.

(Waugh *The Limping Pilgrim*, 1882)

These extracts show two things: firstly that the islanders had to make use of every available resource, secondly how precarious their lives were. If these resources failed, or could not be taken advantage of, then there was nothing to fall back upon. The islanders lacked the capital to invest and create an industry; they could only gather the windfalls of nature. This was sufficient as long as there was a balance between population and resources. For most island history there was, though cruelly administered by nature, famine and war. It was broken in the eighteenth century, firstly by an explosion of population, latterly by an explosion of expectation.

2

Early Christianity

THE SMALL ISLES HAVE a particularly rich Early Christian tradition. For the west coast the label Early Christian implies the activities of the various missionary saints in the period 500 to 800 AD. I am also going to touch on the subsequent period of Viking settlement because of the remarkable crosses in Eigg and Canna.

Attention has frequently been drawn to the fact that, after the fall of the Roman Empire, Christianity survived and spread again from the west. The vitality and asceticism of these Early Christians, as well as their artistic achievements, made a critical contribution to Western culture. However, historians of this process have had their own agendas and there is much debate about the nature of what is referred to as 'Celtic Christianity'. I am not going to discuss 'Celtic Christianity', or the work of any of these early churchmen, except in the context of the Small Isles. If we confine ourselves to the facts then others can supply whatever conceptual or religious glosses they wish.

Early Christianity on the west coast was primarily Irish in origin and impetus, even if it was quickly absorbed and integrated by native peoples. However, Irish does not necessarily mean Columban. The later ecclesiastical primacy of Iona, and its domination of the literary record, tends to obscure contributions from elsewhere. Within the Irish sphere there were different traditions: that of Columba, those of Moluag and Maelrubha. Not all the early Christian saints were Irish, there were also Britons and Picts. Finally, some of the sculptural associations suggest links with Argyll, Whithorn and Man, rather than just Iona. The progress of early Christianity up the west coast was much more diverse, the contemporary scene much more of a melting-pot, than presently appears.

The Dalriadic Scots from Northern Ireland founded their colonies in Argyll and the Southern Hebrides from about 500 AD. A base-line is established in the religious record by St Columba's foundation of the monastery of Iona in 563. In 672 St Maelrubha set up his monastery at Applecross. Between these two dates we can argue for the conversion of the Small Isles and their integration into the world of Irish monasticism.

This was not a simple process. The Dalriadic Scots were invaders whose relationship with the indigenous peoples of the west coast is uncertain. In Argyll they settled and conquered. North of Ardnamurchan the process is speculative. They certainly converted, but quite how the Pictish and Dalriadic worlds became integrated is debatable. Conversion may have proceeded hand-in-hand with dynastic intermarriage and local patronage. In Raasay we find the place-name Kilmaluag and some fine early carved stones. These suggest St Moluag preceded St Donnan in the area and established a presence in Raasay between about 563 and 592. The patronage of a Pictish dynasty in Skye may explain his success. Possibly Eigg fell within the bounds of a different magnate who decided to patronise Donnan.

We have different types of evidence for the Early Christian period in the Small Isles: monastic records, poetry, place-names, archaeology and sculpture. There is also the legacy of custom and tradition.

Documentary evidence

The following accounts are all taken from A. O. Anderson's *Early Sources of Scottish History*:

> The burning of Donnan of Eigg, on the fifteenth before the Kalends of May, with a hundred and fifty martyrs.
>
> > (*Annals of Tigernach* referring to
> > 17 April 618(?))

This is also in the *Annals of Ulster* for 616 (= 617).

> Great Donnan and his monks . . . The number of their congregation was 52, and the sea-pirates came to the island where they were and killed them all. The name of that island is Ego.
>
> > (*Martyrology of Gorman*, 17 April)

> Donnan of Eigg, i.e. Eigg is the name of an island in Scotland . . . and St Donnan died there with his community, fifty-five.
>
> This Donnan is he who went to Columcille, to take him for his confessor. And Columcille said to him, 'I will not be a confessor,' said he, 'to people who are to suffer violent martyrdom; for thou shalt enter violent martyrdom, and thy community with thee.' And that is what was fulfilled. Donnan went after that among the Gall-gaidil, and took up his abode in the place where the queen of the country's sheep used to be. This was told to the queen. 'Kill them all' said she. 'That is not devout' said the others.

Thereafter men go to them, to kill them. The priest was then at mass. 'Grant us peace till the mass is ended' said Donnan. 'We will' said they. Thereafter they were all killed, as many as were there.

(*Martyrology of Oengus*, 17 April)

Anderson adds: 'Of the above, only the sentence that says that Donnan died in Eigg is in Latin; the rest, in Irish, is a different account and is fabulous'.

Donnan of Eigg, abbot. Eigg is the name of an island in which he was after he left Ireland. And sea-robbers came one time to the island, while he was celebrating mass; he begged them not to kill him till he had concluded the mass; and they gave him this favour. And afterwards he was beheaded, and 52 of his monks along with him. And all their names are in a certain old book of the books of Ireland. AD 616.

(*Martyrology of Donegal*, 17 April)

Reeves gave the date of Donnan's martyrdom as 17 April 617. Monastic life on Eigg could have resumed fairly quickly. St Beccan may have been a hermit in Rum as early as 632 or 633 and it is quite likely that Eigg and Rum then shared the same overlord, as they were to do for much of their later history. In the light of the story of St Donnan being beheaded Martin Martin's description is intriguing.

About thirty yards from the church there is a sepulchral urn under ground; it is a big stone hewn to the bottom, about four feet deep, and the diameter of it is about the same breadth; I caused them to dig the ground above it, and we found a flat thin stone covering the urn: it was almost full of human bones, but no head among them, and they were fair and dry. I inquired of the natives what was become of the heads, and they could not tell; but one of them said, perhaps their heads had been cut off with a two-handed sword, and taken away by the enemy.

> (Martin *A Description of the Western Islands of Scotland*, *c.* 1695)

Beccan of Rum reposed in the island of Britain.

> (*Annals of Tigernach*, *c.* 677)

Beccan's death is also reported in the *Annals of Ulster* for 677 whilst the *Annals of the Four Masters* give the date as 17 March. The Irish annals tell us of later religious figures in Eigg:

> Eogan, abbot of Eigg, died.
>
> > (*Annals of Ulster*, *c.* 725)

> Cummine . . . the religious of Eigg, died.
>
> > (*Annals of Tigernach*, 752)

Even if Eigg was not a Columban foundation, close contact seems to have been maintained between the various Early Christian groups. There is a reference in Adomnan's *Life of St Columba* to Columba's foster son Baithene being detained by contrary winds in Eigg. These prevented him from sailing to join Columba in Hinba. Baithene succeeded Columba as abbot of Iona and there is a nice story touching his resolution.

> And what is more difficult, at harvest-time when he was carrying to the stack a sheaf collected in his [one] hand, he meanwhile raised the other to the sky, and appealed to the Thunderer; and in his devotion did not remove the midges that settled on his face.
>
> > (*Life of Baithine*)

Perhaps this trial took place in Eigg. It is not recorded whether Beccan faced a yet sterner test in Rum.

Isobel Henderson and John Bannerman have drawn attention to records of western Pictish families which found their way into the Irish monastic chronicles. We know of a dynasty from Skye who travelled to Ireland in 668 and returned two years later. Their embassy suggests some form of political or religious clientship. Why would they go unless they were in some way supplicant or tributary?

We know there was considerable disruption and dislocation around 672. The Picts were defeated by the Angles. The Pictish king Drust was expelled. In 673 Applecross was established. We do not have enough evidence to be sure of the relationship between Scots and Picts in the west but there may well have been some sort of political settlement. Whether there was a vacuum, into which the Scots stepped, or whether Applecross was the price of Scottish support, they seem to have leap-frogged up the coast. The evidence suggests the eclipse, or accom-modation, of the principal Pictish dynasty in the area. Intermarriage and conversion may have been important contributory factors.

We can see a process behind the events charted in the monastic chronicles. In 563 Iona was close to the frontline. (One interpretation of the story about Columba's supposed refusal to be Donnan's soul-friend or confessor is that Eigg was then regarded as hostile territory and there-fore too dangerous for a monastery.) However if Eigg was a frontier in 617 it was well behind it by the time of Maelrubha's death in 722. Adomnan, who died in 704, refers to the then frontier as *dorsum Britanniae* (the spine of Britain), which implies the mountainous watershed to the east of the western coastline.

We can draw parallels between the process of Dalriadic expansion and the establishment of Viking colonies two centuries later. Both peoples came by sea in a period when sea travel was the principal means of communication. Coming by sea they could dominate island communities who could not quickly be reinforced by each other or from the mainland. This begs the question of whether Scottish naval technology was either inherently superior to that of the Picts, or became so. Certainly the southern Hebrides are richer than the northern and it may be that after a century in Argyll the curraghs of the Scots could overcome those of the Picts of the north-west.

Adomnan's boundary is a telling description and is supported by analogy with the Vikings. The limit of Norse expansion was also the watershed to the east of the western sea-lochs. Within the area known as the Rough Bounds there are three examples of *Coire nan Gall* (Foreigners' Corrie) in a north–south line at the inner end of three major loch-drainage systems (Duich, Nevis and Morar). At the time of Adomnan's abbacy of Iona (679–704) the Dalriadic colonisation of the west coast may have paralleled that of the Norse two centuries later, although power and settlement flowed from the south rather than the north.

Poetry

The other form of written evidence for the early church on the west coast is poetry. Clancy and Markus have retranslated some of the early poetry connected with Iona and draw attention to the work of Beccan mac Luigdech. We cannot be certain, but there are grounds for believing this Beccan to be the same Beccan who was a hermit on Rum and died in 677. He was a conservative on the controversial issue of the dating of Easter and in 632 or 633 a famous letter arguing the Roman position was addressed to him and Abbot Segine of Iona.

His poetry certainly expresses a familiarity with sea-travel. Here he writes of St Columba:

He left Ireland, entered a pact,
he crossed in ships the whales' shrine.
He shattered lusts – it shone on him –
a bold man over the sea's ridge.

He fought wise battles with the flesh,
indeed, he read pure learning.
He stitched, he hoisted sail tops,
a sage across seas, his prize a kingdom.

Prosperous, numerous, safely,
a storm blew them in boats over brine.

(Clancy and Markus (eds), from *Fo Reir
Choluimb* in *The Earliest Poetry of Iona*)

in scores of curraghs with an army of wretches he crossed
the long-haired sea.
   He crossed the wave-strewn wild region, foam-flecked,
seal-filled, savage, bounding, seething, white-tipped,
pleasing, doleful.

(Clancy and Markus (eds), from *Tiugraind
Beccain* in *The Earliest Poetry of Iona*)

Such poems introduce us to the extraordinary force and
intensity of Christianity as experienced by these early Irish
monks. They display a tenacity and a single-mindedness
which has always fascinated later observers. Lots of retrospective interpretations have been put upon this 'Celtic
Christianity', but in the context of Beccan, hermit of Rum,
we can stress the following.

There was a yearning for solitariness, for physical
isolation, for simplicity – these men needed a remote or
desert place. There was an admiration for scholarship,
for learning, for intellectual rigour – such men set themselves mental as well as physical challenges. There was a
conviction that, in order to attain higher levels of spiritual

achievement, the needs of the body had to be overcome or sublimated. Hence the asceticism, fasting and chastity; the denial of comfort, food and sex.

The eremitic tradition – the desire to be a hermit – has always been part of Western monasticism and survives even today. To go off and live as a solitary, to commune alone with God, has been regarded as the final and fullest expression of the monastic ideal. It has a long history, from the desert fathers of Egypt to those who went off to find or create their particular desert in the western seas. Throughout the Hebrides and Northern Isles, even the Faeroes and Iceland, there are traces of these vagrant Early Christians. The word desert has itself passed into Gaelic and features in place-names such as Dysart.

The eremitical approach ran alongside the coenobitic or community form of monasticism with which we are more familiar. The two strands are intertwined throughout the early history of missionary endeavour on the west coast. Beccan the hermit (or *solitarius* as he is described), seems to have had a particular connection with Rum, the largest but geographically the harshest of the Small Isles.

There are three sites with Early Christian associations in Rum; Kilmory in the north, Bagh na h-Uamha on the east coast and Papadil in the south. The first is a settlement site, the probable location of the mediaeval chapel, and has two early Christian stones. Bagh na h-Uamha has a cross-marked slab while the only reason we assume Papadil has a religious connection is its name: it derives from Norse *Papar-dalr* (priests' dale).

In terms of remoteness Papadil is the most likely refuge for Beccan. Kilmory is a more favourable location and probably always had some sort of lay community. Bagh na h-Uamha has a cave large enough for occupation whilst the cross-marked slab was retrieved from the beach below.

Papadil is remote and isolated, perhaps the most appealing for a true hermit. However, if Beccan lived on Rum for forty years then it is quite possible that he had some association with all three sites.

Beccan's poetry does not allude directly to Rum but it does shed light on the cultural milieu into which Rum had recently been drawn. It is clear from the analysis by Clancy and Markus that the poet had great technical skill. The form of the poem is demanding and contrived. There is an elaborate rhyming scheme and plenty of alliterative device; the language is ferociously intellectual and laden with symbolism. Beccan had an agenda. He wished to draw attention to particular aspects of Columba, his asceticism, his clarity of thought and his social position. There is nothing of compromise or woolly-mindedness here; this is not pick-and-mix religion. This is an intellectual tour-de-force, motivated by a fierce and intense faith. Everything is rational, except perhaps for a common clerical blind-spot about visions and dreams, and of course, the religious impulse itself.

Place-names

Place-names provide a generalised proof of an Early Christian presence although, like all names, they are liable to corruption. Even if such sites are not always attested in early documents they can at least suggest associations. In particular, names beginning with *kil-* (from *cille*, cell or church) have long been linked with the spread of the Early Christian church. They are especially thick in Kintyre which is the closest point to Ireland. A lot of kil-names in the Highlands are associated with early missionaries rather than with persons from scripture. Much energy therefore has been expended in trying to map their distribution.

In Eigg we have Kildonnan – the church of Donnan, in Muck and Canna we simply have A' Chill – the church. Martin Martin (1695) tells us that the church in Canna was dedicated to St Columbus (Columba). In Muck a field by the graveyard was called Dail Chill Fionain. There was more than one Finnan but it is likely to be the same man who is remembered in St Finnan's Isle, Loch Shiel, in the neighbouring mainland of Moidart.

In Rum we have the place-name Kilmory which is problematic. Sometimes, as in Kilmory, Arisaig, we find early spellings like Kilmaroy which prove that the name derives from St Maelrubha. Unfortunately we have no early spellings for Kilmory in Rum which could help pin down its origin. The best we have are *Kilmoir* and *Kilmore* from Macfarlane which probably represent Timothy Pont's notes made in the 1590s. There are several dedications to St Maelrubha along the west coast and this is perhaps the most likely option. However we have a Kilmorie or Cill Mhairi on the north side of Ardnamurchan, and another at Laudale in Morvern, which could be dedicated to the Virgin Mary instead.

We do not find *annat* (mother-church) although perhaps we should not expect to in these small islands; we do, however, find Papadil in Rum. This tells us that at some time during the Norse period this corner of south-west Rum was home to some priests or monks. Given the remoteness of the site and the lack of material evidence they may in fact have been solitaries or hermits whose simple lives have left no trace.

Physical evidence

The physical evidence is of two types, archaeological and sculptural. The two principal sites are at A' Chill, Canna, and Kildonnan, Eigg. These were well chosen in terms of their proximity to good agricultural land. Unfortunately this also means the areas have been well cultivated ever since and traces of any Early Christian establishments are hard to find.

Canna

Canna evidently belonged to the monastery of Iona because it is mentioned in a papal bull of 1203. In view of the dedication to Columba and the continued Norse patronage of the site it seems reasonable to suppose that the island had belonged to Iona from as early as the seventh century. Just as conditions in the last quarter of the seventh century allowed St Maelrubha to establish the community at Applecross, so the Columban family on Iona may have grasped the opportunity to found further houses in the Hebrides, for instance in Canna and at Loch Chalumcille in Trotternish, Skye. According to the Irish annals, Iona was given as an offering by Conall, King of Dalriada, in 574. In the same way we can assume that other sites up the west coast were ceded by local magnates in propitiation of this new and powerful religion coming from the south.

There are two stone crosses in Canna and a number of cross-marked slabs.

Canna 1 (see Plates 1 and 2). This is a famous and elaborate cross which probably still stands in its original base on the original site. The face of the cross illustrates the Adoration of the Magi, a horseman and animal scenes. Some of the carving is in very high relief. The carving on the reverse is flatter and the opposing beasts in one of the panels invite parallels with the cross at Eilean Mor, Argyll, which is thought to be tenth-century.

Canna 2 (see Plates 3b, 3c and 4). This is an extraordinary stone which has drawn much less attention than it should. Not everybody regards it as a cross but there do appear to be armpits for a disc at the top. On the reverse are three panels, the uppermost contains a key pattern, the middle interlace, while the bottom one shows intertwined creatures with serpentine bodies, fish tails and animal heads. These panels and motifs can be paralleled on Pictish sculptures elsewhere in Scotland.

On the obverse is the figure of a man with his legs splayed and his arms set saltire-wise across his chest. He wears a short tunic, decorated with a double triquetra, beneath which is disappearing a beak-headed serpent. This must be a symbolic motif, presumably with some sort of sexual significance, but what?

Carola Hicks has compared this with a scene on the front panel of the cart from the ninth-century Oseberg ship-burial in Norway. This is thought to represent Gunnar in the snake-pit. The Canna stone is usually dated to the ninth or tenth century and so a Viking source is perfectly possible; however the treatment is very different. The figure on Canna appears monumental, not decorative. It could be argued that the symbolism has Christian meaning with the serpent being trampled underfoot, but on the Canna slab it is by no means obvious that the human figure is victorious. If the stone is a cross and if the figure represents Christ then some explanation is required for the ritual set of the arms and the attitude of the serpent.

As for style the only stone I have seen which offers a parallel is a carved slab from Waldenbuch, Württemberg, in Germany (see Plate 3a). This has a similar scene on both faces but was carved several centuries earlier. It is just possible that Canna's subject-matter is shared with Waldenbuch and drawn from a Germanic myth also carried by the Vikings. The parable must have had meaning for a contemporary audience and some well-known legend is a likely source. It is also possible that the Canna slab could, like the Pictish slab on Eigg, have had its faces carved at different dates. The reverse of the slab is flat whilst the front has an outward curve. The style and subject matter of the face of this cross are unique.

There are five more cross-marked slabs in the graveyard and a further five are in Canna House. These show a range of designs. Some crosses are Latin, some Greek, some have expanded terminals, some bifurcated. This variety adds to the complexities of dating. Perhaps the most interesting is a stone which shows a Maltese cross within a disc. This is matched in Rum and, with some variation, in Muck. In both Canna and Rum the cross has a handle or stem, like the one in Raasay (see Plates 5 and 6 and Figure 1).

Whatever the origin of the compass-drawn designs I do not believe the crosses on Rum or Canna were ever supposed to represent flabella or liturgical fans. They may share their motifs with flabella – they may even have been inspired by them – but essentially they show a crucifix on stone. The distinctive handles or stems of these fans are certainly a strong argument that they were borrowed as decorative devices. Nevertheless the carvings in the Small Isles are primarily about the Christian symbols created by intersecting circles – the triquetra (Trinity) or Maltese Cross (crucifix). The hexafoil can be seen as a refinement of this; hexafoils can however occur without stems, as at St Ciaran's Cave, Achinhoan, Kintyre.

Sgorr nam Ban-naomha

There are the remains of an Early Christian cashel, or enclosed monastic site, at Sgorr nam Ban-naomha (Sgorr

CROSSES
OF
ARCS

These designs are all compass drawn.

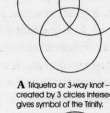

A Triquetra or 3-way knot – created by 3 circles intersecting – gives symbol of the Trinity.

B Four circles intersecting, and enclosed by a fifth the same size. The spaces between the intersections give a Maltese cross. The intersections have squared ends as in Muck.

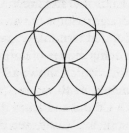

C As B, but with a larger enclosing circle to give complete ovals at the intersections.

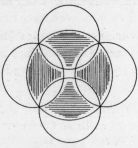

D A more realistic Maltese cross-shape is achieved if the circles are set slightly apart. The centre is filled with a small circle in Raasay and Rum.

E By intersecting 6 circles (+ 1 to enclose) we make a hexafoil or marigold cross of which there are a number of examples in Argyll.

Figure 1

of the Holy Women) on the south-west coast of Canna. J. L. Campbell has pointed out that Sgorr should be translated in the Faeroese sense of a grassy slope between cliffs, which is perfectly descriptive of the site. Its Early Christian associations are proven by its name and the fact that three cross-slabs have been found here.

It measures about 39 m by 32 m and is enclosed by a wall about 1.8 m thick. Inside the wall are a number of ruinous structures. Without full archaeological excavation there is perhaps not a great deal more that can be sensibly said, except to draw attention to the plumbing arrangements. There is a stone-lined and lintelled conduit leading from 'the well-house' to 'the mill'. According to J. L. Campbell this was frequently cleared out 'in the old days' by locals who revered the site. Only excavation will establish the proper functions of these various structures but there are plenty of possible parallels with bath-houses, sweat-houses and so on, in both Scottish and Irish contexts. There is another cashel at Loch Chalumkille, Trotternish, Skye.

The Revd J. Somerville visited the site in about 1898 and writes of a structure called 'The Altar':

> Near it is a flagged underground passage, about 2 feet in width, up which sick people used to crawl to a spring of water. Having done this, they were laid in a *leaba* or bed made of stones, and left there for the night, in the expectation that cure would certainly follow.

Professor MacPherson sent Somerville some additional information drawn from a former Canna resident:

> The people held it in great veneration, and on Sundays when there was no priest on the island, the Tarbert people went there to say their prayers. They told us of the sick who used to be brought there to be cured and left in a

> '*leaba crabhach*'. As far as I remember, there were four or
> five of these beds; . . . The people of the island used to
> speak of nuns being there at one time.

It is difficult, at this distance, to build too much on such anecdotes but we have the following interconnected themes: an Early Christian site within a wall, a name which suggests a connection with women, a reputation for healing and what appears to be a fairly sophisticated water supply. The site is remote; land access is difficult and dangerous, so the main form of access must always have been by sea. The site is big enough for a community, but evidently this community was not part of the economic landscape. They depended on being supplied by boat, but kept any outside interest both distant and minimal. All these themes reinforce the probability that this cashel was occupied by women; moreover, these women worked within an organised institutional framework.

Hinba?

J. L. Campbell thought Canna might have been Hinba, a hitherto unidentified monastic site which is referred to several times in Adomnan's *Life of Columba*. A number of other islands have also been proposed for Hinba, including Jura, Gunna and Colonsay/Oronsay. I do not believe we have enough evidence to make this identification yet. Any proposal rests on too many questionable assumptions. Canna has one theoretical disadvantage and one concrete advantage.

The disadvantage is that if we accept Canna as Hinba then the Columban advance went much further up the west coast much earlier than is normally envisaged. The advantage is that the substantial number of cross-slabs on Canna suggest that it really was a very important Early Christian site.

Rum

Kilmory is a favoured settlement site and amidst the ruins of the old clachan is a small burial-ground which contains two interesting stones. One is a thin pillar with a neatly carved 'cross-of-arcs' on one face. The other is ostensibly a grave-marker with a recent inscription but its cruciform shape strikes me as early. It is common to find stones reused in Highland graveyards where need and ignorance of a slab's previous history encouraged 'borrowing'. The form of this stone is reminiscent of some of the slabs at Skellig Mhicheil, Ireland, which have rounded heads and truncated arms. T. S. Muir must also have been struck by the outline of this stone because he includes a sketch of it in his *Ecclesiological Notes* although he says nothing about its potential age in the text.

The other Early Christian stone in Rum is a pillar-slab at Bagh na h-Uamha. Here an imposing cave overlooks a sandy beach. The pillar-stone is marked with a cross, originally Greek, the shaft of which was lengthened to make it Latin. It was found below high water-mark some years ago, dragged back to dry ground and re-erected. The cave may once have sheltered a hermit. Certainly caves were occupied by Early Christians, as well as lots of other groups of people, when occasion or need demanded. Several caves have strong religious associations, like St Ciaran's Cave, Achinhoan, Kintyre, or St Columba's Cave, Cove, by Loch Caolisport, Knapdale.

Eigg

In Eigg the early monastery was possibly inside the fort at Rubha na Crannaig although there is no hard evidence for this. There are a number of stones in Eigg Lodge which presumably came from the monastery (see Plates 5 and 6).

There is a small broken stone showing a Greek cross, with bifurcated terminals, within a ring, and there are triquetras between the cross-arms.

There are two slabs with enigmatic carvings which may have once been linked. They have been described as cross-slabs although there is no compelling evidence of Christian symbolism. The carving on one stone seems to end in a sort of spike which may have been a device for fixing into the ground. There is a comparable spike at the foot of the cross on the Pictish cross-slab (see Plate 6).

There is a small kite-shaped stone, now broken, which bears a Greek cross in low relief.

The most intriguing stone on Eigg is the cross-slab with a Pictish carving on one face and an elaborate, interlace-filled cross on the other. The slab is broken and there is a section missing from the middle. In addition the Pictish carving is pretty worn so interpretation must be cautious.

At left is a horseman whose horse rears on his back legs. Above and below are dogs, the top one has a very high abdominal arch like a greyhound. In front of the dog at bottom is a bird (either a goose or eagle) which looks backwards. Then there are two large animals which are presumably bulls and in front of them what is probably a horse and some sort of maned creature. At first sight this looks like a hunt or chase, because of the horseman and dogs, but it may in fact be more in the nature of a procession of animals since those beasts being followed are not deer. The stone contains no classic Pictish symbols but the content and style are unmistakably Pictish. Dating is more difficult.

If we associate the stone with Kildonnan, which is likely, then do we date it prior to the arrival of St Donnan before 597, which would make it extremely early? Otherwise its low relief might suggest early eighth century, by which time Eigg had been Christian for over a hundred years. What is striking is the fact that the stone was made acceptable to Christians by secondary carving. Theoretically of course the Pictish face could have been carved at any time before about 800 and then rededicated during the Viking period. However the stone doesn't fit easily into a supposed sequence of pagan Pict, Christian Scot, Viking.

How was it rededicated? Firstly the stone was reorientated. The Pictish scene on what is now the reverse is at right-angles to the cross on the obverse which was probably carved later. At some stage a Greek cross was incised into the middle of the Pictish scene. Some time afterwards this Greek cross seems to have had one arm extended to turn it into a Latin cross. This is now orientated the same way as the cross on the other face. By such methods the stone, which presumably still had meaning for the local population, was not destroyed but overcome. Its symbolic force was cancelled or subsumed within a Christian context.

Glen Charadail

At the very head of Glen Charadail there is a cluster of small cells at the foot of a steep gully leading down from Lochan Nighean Dughaill. There is absolutely nothing to prove that these have an Early Christian context but there are several features that are striking.

1. Their setting: They are remote, well-concealed and tightly clustered. They are not in the open situation one might expect of a traditional shieling site which, by definition, was set beside an expanse of pasture for cattle. At the risk of subjectivity this simply doesn't look like a shieling site. It is above the grazing which

lies in the more open ground further down the burn. The huts are strong and closely built. They give the impression of a permanent settlement rather than a temporary summer habitation.

2. Their plumbing arrangements. The bed of the stream appears to run beneath the cells and, to my mind at least, there is something artificial about the way in which the burn leaves the loch above. This level of civil engineering suggests an institutional basis.

3. Their construction. The cells were corbel-built, that is, the roof was of stone and not wood and turf. By itself this is not proof of an early date. There are more than 400 shielings in Rum, many of them corbel-built. Since some are only recently derelict it seems that the practice of corbel-building survived until modern times in the Small Isles, perhaps because of a shortage of wood. Nevertheless Glen Charadail is reminiscent of the corbel-built beehive cells in the Garvellochs (Loch Linnhe), or Skellig Mhicheil (Ireland). Such cells were a hallmark of the early church in the west.

4. A short distance above Lochan Nighean Dughaill, and draining into it, is a loch called Loch nam Ban Mora or Loch of the Big Women. This has a tiny island dun a few yards offshore. The fact of a loch with this name being so close to a possible Early Christian site provokes speculation as to whether it housed a female community.

There was also a curious sea-taboo at work in the Small Isles which meant that none of the four islands could be called by their proper names at sea. Eigg was referred to as Eilean nam Ban Mora (Isle of the Big Women). Obviously this was regarded as an important identifying characteristic.

None of these factors is individually conclusive but they do have a cumulative force. We can then draw parallels with Sgorr nam Ban-naomha in Canna:

• Both sites are remote and isolated.
• Neither site is directly linked to agriculture, unlike the monastery at Kildonnan. Both depended on support from outside.
• Both have a sophisticated system of water supply.
• Both are associated with women through place-names.

The link with women and the attention to a pure water supply prompt a further association with Adomnan, Abbot of Iona from 679 to 704. First, Adomnan had an enlightened attitude towards women compared with some of his contemporaries. It found expression in the Cain Adomnan which gave Iona's protection to women. There is a story in *The Martyrology of Oengus* about how Adomnan and his mother were passing a place where a battle was being fought:

> Now Ronait, Adomnan's mother, happened to see a woman with an iron hook in her hand dragging another woman from the opposite side, with the hook fastened in her breast. For men and women used to fight in battle alike at that time. Thereupon Ronait sat down, and said: 'Thou shalt not take me from this place until women are freed forever from this condition, and from battles and campaigns'. So Adomnan promised this thing.
>
> Then there happened to be a great council in Ireland, and Adomnan went to that council with men chosen from the priests of Ireland, and he freed women there.

Gilbert Markus has pointed out that Adomnan's *Life of Columba* is a platform for Adomnan's own concern for the plight of women: the killing of a young girl is avenged, a girl slave is set free, childbirth is eased and so on.

There is also good evidence that the Iona monks in general, and Adomnan in particular, were concerned with issues of cleanliness. The Canons of Adomnan are a collection of twenty regulations concerning clean and unclean food. Although they have always been attributed to Adomnan we have no direct proof they were written by him. However we can show that they were particularly relevant to the Highlands and Islands. Some deal directly with the question of when food is polluted; others with when 'windfall' foods can be consumed. Such situations included sea creatures cast ashore, animals found drowned or half dead after attacks by other animals, and so on. In a harsh environment these were important issues. In a Highland context the loss of cows to 'bone-break', as it was called, was still a significant factor in the eighteenth century. It was important to know whether such animals could still be eaten. However, in a ruling that appears equally relevant to the Highlands, cattle that had been stolen were to be rejected.

Two or three of the regulations could be construed as referring to animals killed by hunting dogs and there is a specific reference to stags being caught in traps. Hunting is covered in a later chapter but it is worth noting that some Hebridean islands, like Rum and Jura, may have been maintained expressly as hunting reserves during the mediaeval period. Adomnan's Canons raise the possibility that they may have had this function for hundreds of years previously as well. Three of the Canons refer to pigs. Given that Muck's name means pig, and that the island may have been owned by Iona from Adomnan's day, it is possible that it was maintained as a piggery for the monastery. If so then these regulations cover issues that may have been raised there. Finally there is one regulation that determines what to do with a well in which a human or animal corpse is found: the well is to be emptied and cleaned.

Such rules are sensible practice for any community. Attention must be paid to the communal supply of food and water or the consequences can be swift and dire. It took material form in the plumbing arrangements in Canna and Eigg. There is a parallel to this on a cross-slab found in Maughold, Man. It has been dated to the early ninth century and commemorates one Branhui who apparently built the water supply system. In the Small Isles there was a severe decline in hygiene in subsequent centuries although the absence of monastic, or any other sizeable communities, meant it became relatively less important.

The Small Isles in the period *c.* 580–800 AD were a centre for Christian activity. Two aspects of this were a respect for women and attention to cleanliness. Clean water also had an important symbolic function which is well-rehearsed in contemporary documents. As fire tested so water cleansed and purified, concepts that reached deep into the Christian consciousness.

Muck

We know that Muck belonged to Iona although it is not listed in the Papal Bull of 1203. Unfortunately its small size has meant it generally escaped documentary attention so we know little of its early history. In later times it is regularly referred to as belonging to the Bishop of the Isles who held the former Iona estate. The only evidence for the early church is slight. There are the ruins of a burial ground near the pier and two Early Christian stones have been found here.

There is a burying-ground with remains of ecclesiastical buildings on the island, but the name of the saint to whom they were dedicated has been forgotten. The place is called simply "A Chill". Probably Kilfinan was the full name, as there is Dail Chill Fionain beside the burying-ground.

(Robertson, 'Topography and Traditions of Eigg' 1898)

For a small group of islands the surviving material evidence is very remarkable. We have a monastery and possibly two nunneries, a Pictish/Christian cross-slab on Eigg and two ninth- or tenth-century crosses on Canna. There are at least twenty-one more Early Christian stones: thirteen on Canna, three on Rum, three on Eigg and two on Muck and no doubt others are lost or concealed. Cumulatively these indicate a strong Early Christian presence and purpose in the Small Isles (see Map 3).

This is not coincidental. Islands were attractive to the early church for a number of reasons. They were secure, and distant from worldly distractions. Men, and women, could live simply and frugally here: had to in fact. R.G. Lamb has pointed out the correlation between small, eremitic stack-sites in the Northern Isles and the available supply of sea-birds. Since the occupants of Sgorr nam Ban Naomha and Glen Charadail were not farming they either had to live on supplies brought from outside or they had to gather their own food. Eggs, sea-birds and shellfish are obvious resources, particularly for the Canna nunnery.

Furthermore, many islands in Britain were considered holy long before Christianity arrived here. Islands, as islands, have often been regarded as sacred sites. It may be that the early church on the west coast was grafted on to a substratum of local belief which already held certain islands to be holy. It is also possible that women had a particular status in the Hebrides when they were part of the Pictish dominion. Adomnan may not have been

42

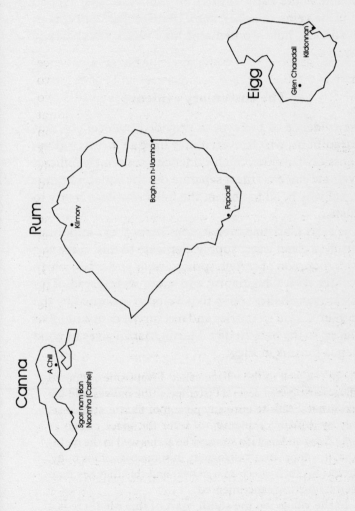

Map 3   Early Christian sites

creating new rights for women so much as responding to rights that already existed. If we take as our premise the notion that the early church on the west coast tapped into prior veins of belief, then perhaps the concepts of holy islands, holy women and holy water were already pervasive.

The customary evidence

More evidence of this type is provided by local customs and traditions, which, even if they have a Christian gloss, are possibly far older. Such evidence is extremely difficult to evaluate since we must separate out the various strands of belief which, all too often, the folklore collectors try to conflate.

The early Christian monasteries knew it was important to ensure a clean water supply. Separate to this, there was also a veneration of certain springs, wells and lakes, which was older than Christianity and more widespread. This substratum of belief seems to have been absorbed by the church in 'Celtic' countries and has survived, in a number of places, to the present day. Martin Martin gives us good evidence for this in Eigg:

> There is a well in the village called Fivepennies, reputed efficacious against several distempers: the natives told me that it never fails to cure any person of their first disease, only by drinking a quantity of it for the space of two or three days; and that if a stranger lie at this well in the night-time, it will procure a deformity in some part of his body, but has no such effect on a native; and this they say hath been frequently experimented. . . .
>
> In the village on the south coast of this isle there is a well, called St Katherine's Well; the natives have it in great esteem, and believe it to be a catholicon for

diseases. They told me that it had been such ever since it was consecrated by one Father Hugh, a Popish priest, in the following manner: he obliged all the inhabitants to come to this well, and then employed them to bring together a great heap of stones at the head of the spring, by way of penance. This being done, he said mass at the well, and then consecrated it; he gave each of the inhabitants a piece of wax candle, which they lighted, and all of them made the dessil, of going round the well sunways, the priest leading them: and from that time it was accounted unlawful to boil any meat with the water of this well.

The natives observe St Katherine's Anniversary; all of them come to the well, and having drank a draught of it, they make the dessil round it sunways; this is always performed on the 15th day of April. . . .

St Donnan's Well, which is in the south-west end, is in great esteem by the natives, for St Donnan is the celebrated tutelar of this isle.

(Martin *A Description of the Western Islands of Scotland*, c. 1695)

There are several ideas contained here. That well-water restores health, that it has different effects on natives compared to strangers, and that it should not be used for certain mundane tasks. The word *fons* (fountain) occurs three times in association with the name Eigg in the early Irish accounts. The wells or springs of Eigg may have had wide repute even in ancient times.

Martin Martin also refers to the old practice of proceeding *deiseal*, or sunwise, around something before commencing a task:

There is a heap of stones here, called Martin Dessil, i.e., a place consecrated to the saint of that name, about which the natives oblige themselves to make a tour round sunways.

This practice proved extremely durable:

> The mound mentioned by Martin as Martin Dessil is well
> known, and the custom referred to of walking round it
> sun-ways was only recently given up.
>
> (Macpherson *Notes on Antiquities*
> *from the Island of Eigg*, 1878)

This habit of performing a sunwise tour applied to
umpteen activities in the Highlands and Hebrides, for
instance before setting off on a journey. In Eigg it also
survived in the practice of taking a sunwise tour around
Kildonnan church before a funeral.

> It is now the burial-place of the Roman Catholic
> inhabitants, whose remains are carried sunwise round the
> outside ere being laid in their last resting-place.
>
> (Robertson 'Topography and
> Traditions of Eigg', 1898)

It was not just in Eigg. Edwin Waugh tells a tale of the old
well at Kilmory. A native of Rum was banished to Coll
where he fell sick and was like to die. He requested some
water from the well at Kilmory as the only thing that could
save him. Unfortunately those who went to fetch it actually
took it from a well that was more conveniently located in
Rum. When they returned to Coll the patient tasted the
water, knew immediately it was not the genuine article,
and expired!

These wells gradually fell out of use, perhaps more
quickly in the Protestant isles than the Catholic. Writing
of the 'White House' in Rum, Edwin Waugh says:

> In a green field behind the house there is a well, strongly
> impregnated with iron and other matters, which are said
> to have a valuable medicinal effect. The well is sunk in the
> field, and there are some traces of rude masonry about its

sides, as if it had been known and used by the old inhabitants of the isle.

(Waugh The Limping Pilgrim, 1882)

Donald M'Lean makes a similar reference in 1794:

> In Rum is a well, called *Tobar Dearg*, (Red Well), the water of which is highly mineral; but very little used by the natives.

In Canna there was a *Tobar Chaluim Chille* and also a *Tobar Mhoire* near the sands of Tarbert.

We should make a conceptual distinction between the beliefs and customs of Celts who practised Christianity in the Early Christian period (which we can never fully know), from those visited upon them by later apologists with their own perceptions of the early church. Now, there is a heavy burden of expectation. 'Celtic' Christianity had, apparently, a much healthier or better attitude to nature than we do; there is a presumption that somehow they were more in tune with their environment.

I am not so sure. It strikes me that the plumbing arrangements evident in both Eigg and Canna have less to do with some idealised simplicity of natural life than with a logical recognition by small communities that unless they ensured a safe, clean, water-supply they would not survive. Theirs was not some woolly-minded compromise with nature; this is a cold, logical and efficiently applied set of communal rules. What we have here is less an attitude that somehow water was sacred than a determination that water must be kept clean. The presumption that the early church was somehow eco-friendly misleads us about its true nature. Such monastic enterprise was driven by ruthless logicality.

Adomnan tells us a story in his *Life of St Columba* which points up this contrast nicely:

> Of a poisonous Fountain of Water to which the blessed man gave his blessing in the country of the Picts.

Again, while the blessed man was stopping for some days in the province of the Picts, he heard that there was a fountain famous amongst this heathen people, which foolish men, having their senses blinded by the devil, worshipped as a god. For those who drank of this fountain, or purposely washed their hands or feet in it, were allowed by God to be struck by demoniacal art, and went home either leprous or purblind, or at least suffering from weakness or other kinds of infirmity. By all these things the Pagans were seduced, and paid divine honour to the fountain. Having ascertained this, the saint one day went up to the fountain fearlessly; and, on seeing this, the Druids, whom he had often sent away from him vanquished and confounded, were greatly rejoiced, thinking that he would suffer like others from the touch of that baneful water. But he, having first raised his holy hand and invoked the name of Christ, washed his hands and feet; and then with his companions, drank of the water which he had blessed. And from that day the demons departed from the fountain; and not only was it not allowed to injure any one, but even many diseases amongst the people were cured by this same fountain, after it had been blessed and washed in by the saint.

(Reeves (ed.) *Life of St Columba*)

In telling this story Adomnan makes a number of points: that some Picts worshipped springs; that those who defiled such water were struck by disease; that Columba tackled this superstition head-on by washing in the water, did not suffer retribution, and then blessed the well which now began to have a healing influence. The worship of wells was pre-Christian; it was not approved of by the Early Christians, but they, like Father Hugh a thousand years later, tried to nullify the threat by absorbing it.

Throughout the Highlands and Hebrides there are faint folk-memories of a myriad of holy wells. They frequently carry saints' names and are often credited with healing powers. Again and again Martin Martin refers to locals who regarded the water of a certain well as a 'catholicon' for all diseases. This said, we do not really know why they were regarded as sacred. They may have been adopted by the early church, they may have been blessed to make them acceptable, but their origins may be pre-Christian.

In Eigg Father Hugh was harnessing a local belief, and the reputation of a particular well, and taking these within the embrace of the church. He was ensuring that any benefits from the well-water flowed to the church as well as the people, thus formalising and making acceptable a quite un-Christian tradition. Who knows how often this was done in earlier times.

Water and fire had enormous symbolic value for the early church, not just as mysterious elements, but as cleansing or testing agents on the road to salvation. We find numerous examples of this in Beccan's poetry. Water for purification has always played a major part in Christian symbolism and iconography.

The Christian church has long practised syncretism, the practice of absorbing and reinventing earlier religious beliefs and customs within a framework that is at least nominally Christian. We are given a sense of just how much was absorbed when we see shocked Reformers fighting not only Catholicism but the vestigial remnants of earlier pagan practice. We have references to bull-sacrifice in Applecross while Martin Martin gives a great many examples of superstitious observance which could never be called Christian. There are two further aspects of island life we can draw attention to here.

The Michaelmas Cavalcade

Martin Martin gives numerous descriptions of island

customs for which we find additional evidence in the Small Isles. He specifically mentions cavalcades in Harris, North Uist, South Uist, Barra, Skye and Tiree. Samuel Johnson describes something similar in Coll while Thomas Pennant tells us the situation in Canna:

> [There were] horses in abundance. The chief use of them in this little district is to form an annual cavalcade at Michaelmas. Every man on the island mounts his horse unfurnished with saddle, and takes behind him either some young girl, or his neighbour's wife, and then rides backwards and forwards from the village to a certain cross, without being able to give any reason for the origin of this custom. After the procession is over, they alight at some public house, where, strange to say, the females treat the companions of their ride. When they retire to their houses an entertainment is prepared with primaeval simplicity: the chief part consists of a great oatcake, called *Struan-Micheil*, or St Michael's cake, composed of two pecks of meal, and formed like the quadrant of a circle: it is daubed over with milk and eggs, and then placed to harden before the fire.

Within a few years of Pennant noting the Canna cavalcade it had been 'broken' by MacNeil, the tacksman, who forbade his people to attend.

Visions and second sight.

Visions make difficulties for Christianity. After all, one man's vision is another man's hallucination. However, like the belief in holy wells, a tolerance for second sight survives, albeit a shadow of its former self. Martin Martin gives an example of second sight in Eigg which, he implies, was borne out in fact. Before the Glorious Revolution an inhabitant of Eigg saw an apparition of a man in a red coat. After Killiecrankie some government troops did indeed pay an unwelcome visit to Eigg. Thomas Pennant though was more sceptical:

> It is not wonderful that some superstitions should reign in these sequestered parts. Second sight is firmly believed at this time. My informant said that Lauchlan MacKerran of Cannay had told a gentleman that he could not rest for the noise he heard of the hammering of nails into his coffin: accordingly the gentleman died within fifteen days.
>
> Molly Macleane (aged forty) has the power of foreseeing events through a well-scraped blade-bone of mutton. Some time ago she took up one and pronounced that five graves were soon to be opened; one for a grown person: the other four for children; one of which was to be of her own kin: and so it fell out. These pretenders to second sight, like the Pythian priestess, during their inspiration fall into trances, foam at the mouth, grow pale, and feign to abstain from food for a month, so overpowered are they by the visions imparted to them during their paroxysms.
>
> I must not omit a most convenient species of second sight, possessed by a gentleman of a neighbouring isle, who foresees all visitors, so has time to prepare accordingly: but enough of these tales, founded on impudence and nurtured by folly.
>
> (Pennant *A Tour in Scotland and Voyage to the Hebrides*, 1772)

Preservation

Dr Samuel Johnson shows himself habitually perceptive on the subject of old customs:

> If we had travelled with more leisure, it had not been fit to have neglected the popish islands. Popery is favourable to ceremony; and among ignorant nations, ceremony is the only preservative of tradition. Since protestantism was extended to the savage parts of Scotland, it has perhaps

been one of the chief labours of the ministers to abolish stated observances, because they continued the remembrance of the former religion. We therefore who came to hear old traditions, and see antiquated manners, should probably have found them amongst the papists.

(Johnson *A Journey to the Western Islands of Scotland*, 1773)

Pennant draws a contrast between the spiritual state of Rum in its earlier and later history:

Here are only the ruins of a church in this island; so the minister is obliged to preach, the few times he visits his congregation, in the open air. The attention of our popish ancestors in this article, delivers down a great reproach on the negligence of their reformed descendants: the one leaving not even the most distant and savage part of our dominions without a place of worship; the other suffering the natives to want both instructor, and temple.

(Pennant *A Tour in Scotland and Voyage to the Hebrides*, 1772)

Religious attitudes have changed since the eighteenth century but the relics of early Christianity in the Small Isles are equally in need of preservation. Carved stones weather and erode. Since they are the only physical remains of a formative period in our culture they deserve especial care.

The Vikings and Christianity

The traditional view of the Vikings is of bloodthirsty warriors who looted and pillaged their way down the west coast and behaved particularly badly towards Christians. Our prime sources for this view are the very same Christian monks who, because their monasteries were repositories of great wealth, were targeted by Vikings and therefore took a rather jaundiced view. There is no doubt that the early raids were accompanied by terrible ferocity. Iona was sacked in 802 and again in 806. Blathmac was martyred there in 825. Nevertheless it is extraordinary how quickly the Vikings became Christian. *Eyrbyggja Saga* has this to say of Bjorn, son of Ketil Flatnose, Lord of the Hebrides at the end of the ninth century:

> By the time that he reached the Hebrides, his father Ketil had died, but he met his brother Helgi and their sisters, and they invited him to share in their prosperity. Bjorn discovered that they'd changed their beliefs and thought it very weak-minded of them to have renounced the old faith of their forefathers; so he didn't take at all kindly to them and wouldn't make his home there
>
> (Palsson and Edwards (eds),
> *Eyrbyggja Saga*, 1973)

Now while this is only saga evidence, the fact that the Vikings quickly adopted the religion of their conquered lands in the Hebrides is confirmed by the cross-marked slabs in a Viking grave in Colonsay. This is important when discussing the two Canna crosses and one face of the Eigg cross-slab.

While the Vikings were struck – indeed converted – by the force of what they came up against, it is still true that the extraordinary religiosity of the Early Christians in the islands was not sustained institutionally. Norse colonisation must have changed the islands sufficiently to subvert the social framework within which Irish monasticism flourished. For somebody like Beccan to write his poetry, for Columba to have the impact he did, there needed to be an institutional framework, sustained by patronage and accommodated within local society. Some of these factors must have been lacking in the Viking period. Iona survived, but it was changed, and had a different relationship to the magnates in the Isles. The church withstood the onslaught, but it was a different sort of church. It still received patronage, but perhaps more for its fabric than its message, its form than its content. The religious communities in Eigg and Canna may not have survived but sculptural patronage certainly did; the finest sculpture in the Small Isles may have been produced during the Viking period.

Dating

It is seldom that we find an Early Christian stone in an archaeological context that we can date exactly. Even when a stone is inscribed it is rare that we can place it very precisely. At best we can date most stones only by means of typology. This means viewing them in their overall sculptural context, trying to define schools of carving, regional variations, traces of influence and so on. Comparisons are made on the basis, among other things, of carving techniques, favoured patterns and styles, symbols and motifs and their pairing and juxtaposition.

Unfortunately type-matching is not an exact science. In fact it can appear highly subjective. Observer A will 'see' a resemblance that escapes Observer B while Observer C is struck by a contrast instead. The problem is compounded by the fact that there is no clear chronology among cross-types. On Iona, for instance, there is a slab which bears four different types of Latin cross. If these were all contemporary how can we hope to establish any sort of retrospective sequence? Moreover, there are hundreds of stones carved in the early Christian period in Scotland alone, let alone the rest of Britain and Ireland, so the process of type-matching is neither complete nor agreed.

What makes matters worse is that in north-west Scotland, chronology and sequence seem particularly irregular. In his book *The Mediaeval Stone Carver in Scotland*, J. S. Richardson wrote:

> This out-of-their-time confusion is common to the plastic art of the West Highlands and Islands, where sculptors seemed to work according to their own old traditions, their works remaining thus throughout the centuries unaffected by the progress of styles and fashions in art and architecture which went on elsewhere in Scotland.

If we accept this premise, and there is certainly plenty of evidence for it in the mediaeval period, then the dating of early sculpture on the west coast becomes a major problem. If we cannot establish sequences or trends in the Highlands then how can we date these early stones? By way of analogy we only have to think how often modern jewellery apes Dark Age Celtic metalwork, or how many ancient Celtic crosses have been carved in recent centuries. There is plenty of controversy about the dating of Pictish sculpture so how exact can we be when dating Christian carvings in the west?

Given that our main analytical tool, type-matching, is notoriously subjective, the problem becomes yet more intractable. Another quotation from Richardson points this up nicely:

> There is a small cross-slab at St Donnan on the Isle of Eigg which has a striking resemblance in character of design and nature of carving to one from Inchbrayock, now in the Museum at Montrose, the resemblance being so strong that one is tempted to suggest that they may be the work of the same school and that the Eigg stone is imported from the East.

> (J. S. Richardson *The Mediaeval Stone Carver in Scotland*, 1964)

Richardson illustrates both stones, and in doing so reveals, to my mind at least, more contrast than likeness!

At the moment the Canna crosses and the Eigg cross-slab are provisionally dated to the ninth or tenth centuries. This means they are post-Viking. Since they occur beside the principal farm-sites at Kildonnan and A Chill it is probable that the leading local family patronised or commissioned them. This does not sit comfortably with our view of the Vikings as violent invaders who obliterated local people and culture. The Viking period will be discussed in the next chapter but for the moment it seems likely that, in the Small Isles, Viking settlers quickly accommodated themselves to local religious practice and became patrons of religious art – perhaps long before their counterparts in Scandinavia.

We know nothing specific about this process but whereas in 800 the Vikings had come as pillagers, by about 1210 they had developed an historical myth to the effect that they had always held Iona sacred! According to *Ingi Bard's Son's Saga* some Norwegians:

> plundered in the Hebrides, and the neighbouring islands . . . They pillaged the holy island [Iona], which Norwegians have always held sacred; then they fell out, and parted . . . And those that came back to Norway were severely rebuked by the bishops for their piracy.

The question of Viking conversion takes us on to the related issue of land-assessment which is dealt with in the next chapter. It is possible that the valuation system that dominated much of the Highlands and Islands for a period of at least 800 years may be older than the Norse invasion. Perhaps the Norse simply lay their assessment system on top of what previously existed. It is a moot point whether, in the context of Eigg, this was a Pictish or Dalriadic substratum.

There are grounds for thinking that, from the time of its institution before 600 AD, Donnan's monastery possessed land to the value of one davach or ounceland; this may well have represented its original endowment, perhaps from a local Pictish magnate to Donnan himself. Theoretically of course it could have existed as a discrete unit for many centuries before that as well. This may be the reason why Kildonnan is the only one of the primary settlement units in Eigg to have retained its pre-Norse name.

There are other religious estates in the Hebrides where we can tell that the old land-assessment value of an ounceland or davach survived intact into at least the mediaeval period. All of these are associated with important churches. An ounceland was a large unit of land but since it was a valuation and not a physical measure, its area depended on its quality.

There are Kilchoman in Islay, the principal church of the Rhinns of Islay; Kirkapoll, Tiree, whose name (Norse: church-farm) suggests the Vikings may have adopted a previously existing unit; and St Columba's Isle, Snizort in Northern Skye. This last was, during the latter stages of Norse rule in the Isles, something like a cathedral church for the Northern Hebrides.

There are very few Pictish symbol stones on the west coast and there is a significant association between their locations and important Christian sites. The symbol stone on Raasay is also carved with an early cross-of-arcs which could be connected with the missionary work of St Moluag in the late sixth century. The reverse of the cross-slab on Eigg is covered with Pictish animals and associated with the site of St Donnan which dates to before the end of the sixth century. The symbol-stone at Tote, Skye, is directly opposite St Columba's church on an island in the River

Snizort. This later became the major church in the Northern Hebrides and its foundation may date back to the seventh century. It is quite possible that these three sites were chosen for Christian establishments because they were already sacred to the Picts.

Sculpture

What light can sculptural associations throw on the religious make-up of the Small Isles? Columba and Maelrubha represented different strands within the Irish church; Donnan of Eigg was unacceptable to Columba for his courting of red martyrdom while Beccan of Rum seems to have been an important religious conservative. So whatever Iona's claims to supremacy, then and since, there was an element of diversity in the early church in the Hebrides. Is this in any way reflected in the sculptural record?

In order to assess this I am going to concentrate on only one aspect of these Early Christian stones and that is the *type* of cross they portray. I shall ignore other factors such as carving techniques, questions of style, shape of slab and so on. There is a great variety of cross-types but for the purpose of this chapter I shall concentrate on three:

- Latin, where the shaft is longer than the other three arms;
- Greek, where the arms are of equal length;
- Maltese, an equal-armed cross where the arms are splayed towards the ends.

One method of creating a Maltese cross was by means of a compass. When art historians use terms like compass-drawn, cross of arcs or Maltese, they are referring to a

technique whereby the shape of the cross was achieved by
intersecting circles. This process is illustrated in Figure 1
(see p. 32). Other designs like hexafoils and triquetras
were made simply by using more or fewer circles. The
two simplest combinations have Christian connotations.
Three circles give a triquetra which can signify the Trinity,
while four circles make a cross. Geometry is also the basis
for interlace.

Compass-drawn crosses were popular locally. We have
two examples on Raasay which were made by intersecting
semi-circles. Both crosses have a handle and one is
accompanied by Pictish symbols. In neither carving do
the semicircles quite meet, which leaves a small space at
the centre of the cross. In one this is filled by a small circle.
In Rum we see exactly the same feature. In both Rum
and Canna the cross has a handle or stem. In Canna and
Muck the intervening sections are truncated as in Figure
1 (B). How does this local group relate to the wider Early
Christian world?

In their recent inventory of Iona the Royal Commission
list seventy-nine Early Christian cross-slabs. Some of these
are worn or fragmentary but about three-quarters of them
carry recognisable Latin crosses. A few show Greek crosses
and only two bear Maltese crosses or crosses of arcs. One
of these, the 'Echoid' stone, is probably seventh century.

The relative frequency of other cross-types such as
Greek and Maltese suggests there was a different sculptural
flavour in the Small Isles. So if it wasn't Iona, where did
the sculptors of the Small Isles get their ideas from? There
are a number of Maltese crosses and hexafoils in Argyll,
Whithorn and particularly the Isle of Man. There are also
examples in Ireland.

We should not read too much into this issue, but the
choice of cross-type and the sources of influence indicate

that Early Christianity in the area was much more of a composite than the later historiography of Adomnan and Iona might suggest. In the early years of missionary activity the Small Isles were subject to artistic and symbolic influence from Argyll, Whithorn and Man as much as from Iona.

The other consideration in favour of local variation is that many of these stones must have been carved on site. The biggest institutions such as Iona and Applecross may have maintained their own sculptors, but there are so many Early Christian stones scattered throughout the West Highlands that many more must have been carved by travelling masons. This would explain the diversity of design, and we can think of sculptural trends cutting across institutional distinctions.

The restricted range of cross-types at Iona and the relatively wide range found in the Small Isles makes me wonder if certain cross-types were, or became, associated with particular movements or factions. The pillar-slab at Bagh na h-Uamha, Rum, bears what was originally a slightly irregular Greek cross. This was later lengthened into a Latin cross. Rum was the stamping-ground of Beccan the hermit, who was a conservative on the thorny question of the dating of Easter. This was a matter of critical importance to the Early Church and Beccan, along with the Abbot of Iona, had received a letter in 632 or 633 setting out the Roman position on the subject.

The incised cross on the 'Pictish' face of the Eigg cross-slab also appears to have been lengthened from a Greek cross into a Latin cross. Is it possible that the Roman position was or came to be associated with the Latin cross? Was it a sign of orthodoxy? This might explain the relative lack of diversity in the cross-types of Iona and the comparative richness found in smaller outposts of

Christianity such as Muck, Eigg, Rum and Canna. Over time these islands slowly came into line or gave up their carving traditions. The type of cross in use and whether or not it had been 'corrected' might serve as a dating tool. Perhaps Latin crosses did not become the norm until the eighth century.

Finally it is worth reinforcing just how remarkable was the sculptural achievement of the Small Isles. In a later chapter I give some population figures for the sixteenth century based on the numbers of fighting men each island could raise. In the Early Christian and Viking period it is unlikely that population figures were wildly different. Assuming household sizes between five and six we can project the likely number of families on each island:

	Population	Families
Canna	84–100	14–20
Eigg	250–300	41–60
Rum	30–35	5–7
Muck	72–80	12–16

Some of these assumptions may not hold. Viking households may have been far bigger. However even with more generous calculations the number of families on three of the islands is still very small. For them to support the creation of two fine crosses in Canna suggests that the island must have been something of a regional religious centre even in Norse times.

3

The Viking Period

THE VIKINGS ARRIVED, WITH some initial brutality, about 800 AD. Their naval superiority meant that the islands quickly fell under their control. To the Irish chroniclers the Hebrides became *Innsegall*, or the Foreigners' Isles. There is considerable debate about the extent of Norse colonisation in Scotland and I am only going to deal with this in so far as it affects the Small Isles. The islands would certainly have been attractive to Norse settlers. They were secure from counter-attack, except by sea, and it was the sea that the Vikings controlled. We have no written records to tell us of their activities here but we do have some archaeological remains, their place-names and their land-assessment system. Using these we can build a picture of what is likely to have happened.

Archaeology

Map 4 shows the archaeological finds in Eigg which have a Viking context. The most important are the graves at

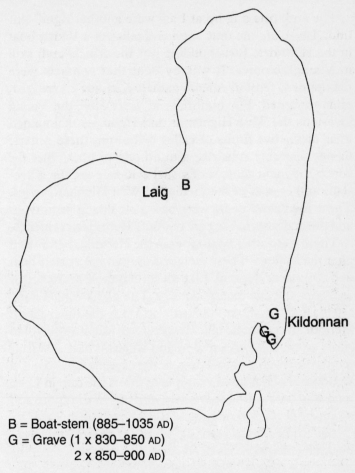

B = Boat-stem (885–1035 AD)
G = Grave (1 x 830–850 AD)
        2 x 850–900 AD)

Map 4   Viking archaeology on Eigg

Kildonnan which are dated to the late ninth century. The relics include a sickle and it is likely that we are dealing with the local Viking chieftain or landowner, someone who had settled permanently.

The endposts dug up at Laig were another significant find. These are the only surviving relics of a Viking boat in the Hebrides. Boat-building was the critical craft skill in Viking colonies. It was by boat that contacts were maintained, reinforcements gathered, goods exchanged, raids mounted. For hundreds of years after the Viking invasions the West Highlands and Hebrides maintained their distinctive forms of galley or birlinn; these generic names probably subsume a multitude of boat-types for which the main sources of visual evidence are the grave-slabs and crosses of the mediaeval West Highland series. These mediaeval boats were based on Viking prototypes and the endposts in Eigg are our only Hebridean evidence.

There were other boat-types in the Hebrides before and after the Vikings. These included the *curragh* or skin-boat and the *amir* or dug-out. Like the birlinn these are recorded as late as the eighteenth century. The plank-built Viking type lasted for about 900 years and was the linch-pin of Hebridean economic life. However, we might expect skin boats to be used on small inland waters where it wasn't worth the trouble of carrying, or the expense of making, a wooden vessel. A good example of this is the dun in Loch nam Ban Mora. It is only a few yards from the shore and a skin-built *curragh* or coracle would have been ideal.

The timbers found at Laig consist of a stem and stern-post, one of which has been carefully stepped to take the run of the strakes. The vessel would have been clinker-built, that is with the strakes overlapping and fixed together by clinch-nails. At the time of discovery there was also a third piece of wood which was not preserved. This might have been a keel. These three timbers, stem-post, stern-post and keel, were the most important in any boat and may have been deliberately buried to preserve them for future use. Almost as interesting is the find-site itself:

Extending from the sea below the farmhouse of Laig is a low tract little above high-water mark, and once a moss. It is about half a mile long from west to east, and about quarter of a mile broad from north to south. It is separated from the sea by a ridge . . . It used to be said that the whole flat was formerly a lake, which the Norsemen used as a winter harbour for their galleys; while a gap in the ridges of shingle, probably an old water channel, was pointed out as the canal by which they drew them to the lake. In confirmation of this theory, a rock was pointed to which is called '*Sron na laimhrig*', or the landing-point. This rock, from the sea, looks quite unimportant, and is not of use either in guiding to a safe anchorage or in enabling any danger to be avoided; but its name derives new meaning from the discovery of the remains of the boat.

(Macpherson *Notes on Antiquities from the Island of Eigg*, 1878)

Twenty years later Robertson writes to the same effect:

About one-third of a mile from the sea, is a dark rock, called Stron Laimhrig – headland of the landing-place. The inference is that there must have been a landing-place near the foot of the rock, and consequently that the sea must have occupied that now inland basin so as to touch such landing-place. A change in the level of the land of 25 feet or 30 feet would fully satisfy the conditions; and that there has been a change of level in the island can be abundantly proved.

(Robertson 'Topography and Traditions of Eigg', 1898)

The idea is that in winter some Viking boats were hauled up out of the reach of the stormy seas. There are other sites in the Hebrides, such as Rubha an Dunain in Skye, where this may also have been practised. Dr M. Jarvis of

Glasgow University has estimated that the dimensions of the Laig boat would have been approximately 10.4 m x 2.05 m. The wood has recently been carbon-dated to the period 885–1035 AD.

Laimhrig is a Gaelic borrowing from a Norse word meaning landing-place. Not only does it provide a clue to Norse practice in Eigg but the name also occurs as a farm near Bagh na h-Uamha on the eastern coast of Rum. This is not the most hospitable coastline but just below the large cave which now gives the beach its name there is a fine stretch of sand which would have been an ideal short-term landing-site for Norse longships. In the cave was found a gaming-piece made of narwhal ivory which has an interlace pattern on one face. Nearby, what is said to have been a Norse kist was found in the 1940s. The conjunction of this type of ivory, the kist and the place-name, suggest a Norse settlement.

Place-names

Map 5 shows us Norse place-names in the islands. Depending upon one's perspective these can be used to argue for or against a significant Norse presence. The names of the islands of Eigg and Rum are, on the evidence of the Irish Chronicles, pre-Norse. Muck is Gaelic but could have been named before or after the arrival of the Norse. Sanday and Heiskeir are Norse but Canna is debatable; we can claim it is pre-Norse because the name Cana appears in the eighth-century Ravenna Cosmography, or Norse because it is often spelled Cannay, which would match a common Norse suffix in the Hebrides.

As with other islands in the Hebrides most place-names were not recorded until comparatively recently but there are particular circumstances that make place-name studies especially difficult in the Small Isles. The population of Eigg was devastated twice in the sixteenth century, once by the Maclean invasion, once by the massacre in Francis' Cave. With one exception every family in Rum was cleared at the beginning of the nineteenth century, long before the Ordnance Survey systematically collected local names for their maps. As a result the place-names in Rum and Eigg may not be as representative as they might be.

Rum illustrates the problem. Almost all the hill-names are Norse, but there is only one clear Norse farm-site – Raonapoll. It could be argued that the Norse named the hills because they were important sea-marks but left the rest of the island to the indigenous Gael. Against this one could claim that Rum's toponymy is distorted by emigration. Or that since Rum was, according to a late sixteenth-century description, only sparsely populated, there were never more than a handful of settlement sites in the Norse period anyway. Besides, of the nine hamlets in Rum which are named on Langlands' map of Argyll in 1801, seven include Norse elements.

There is also debate about just how much significance we should place on settlement as opposed to topographical names. A minimalist perspective would claim that only where we find 'habitative' names such as *bolstadr* (farm), can we *prove* settlement. Anything else merely indicates influence. A more generous view would be that since Norse settlements elsewhere had topographical names why not allow this for Rum?

For these reasons place-name studies can appear a minefield, a graveyard even for the unwary. Progress can be made through a combination of history and linguistics. In Map 5 and the following notes I have merely tried to show what contribution the historian can make.

THE SMALL ISLES

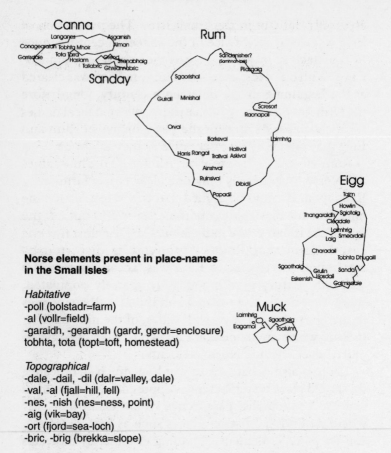

Canna

Langanes
Asgamsh
Conagegatan Tobhta Mhoir Aiman
Garrisdale Tota Tarra Greaq Shenabhaig
Haslam
Tallabric Ghreannabric

Sanday

Rum

Sandanisher?
(Samnnah-bill)
Pladdgaig
Sgaorishal
Guirdil Minishal
Screson
Raonapoll
Orval
Barkeval
Laimhrig
Halival
Harris Rangal Traltival Askival
Ainshval
Ruinsival
Dibidil
Papadil

Eigg
Talm
Howlin
Thangaraidh Sgiotaig
Cleadale
Laimhrig
Laig Smeordal
Charadail
Tobhta Drugaill
Sgaothaig Sanday
Grulin
Eskernish Hosdail
Galmisdale

**Norse elements present in place-names
in the Small Isles**

Muck
Laimhrig Sgaothaig
Eagamol Toalunn

Habitative
-poll (bolstadr=farm)
-al (vollr=field)
-garaidh, -gearaidh (gardr, gerdr=enclosure)
tobhta, tota (topt=toft, homestead)

Topographical
-dale, -dail, -dil (dalr=valley, dale)
-val, -al (fjall=hill, fell)
-nes, -nish (nes=ness, point)
-aig (vik=bay)
-ort (fjord=sea-loch)
-bric, -brig (brekka=slope)

There are a number of elements included in coastal features which I have not placed on the map but which are commonplace around the Small Isles:
sgeir (sker=skerry)
sgor, sgorr (skor=grassy slope between cliffs)
bogha (bodi=reef)

This map is not comprehensive. I have omitted a number of names to avoid clutter. I recommend the appendix on Canna place-names in J. L. Campbell's book; P. Morgan's booklet on the place-names of Rum; and the Revd C. M. Robertson's article on Eigg. (See Bibliography for details.)

Map 5   Norse place-names

Records of local pronunciation and usage can be revealing:

> In Canna, -*skor* or -*sgor* in place-names of Norse origin is
> used in the Faeroese sense of a steep grassy slope between
> two cliffs, one above and one below.
>
> (Campbell *Canna*, 1994)

> As regards Sgurr in that and some other local names as
> they appear in maps, the inhabitants state that there is
> only one Sguirr in Eigg, all the others so called being
> Sgor, usually pronounced Sgòr, owing to shifting of the
> accent.
>
> (Robertson, 'Topography and
> Traditions of Eigg', 1898)

Place-names including *sgor* are found in each of the Small
Isles.

> *cuidh* meaning locally an enclosed field.
>
> (ibid.)

> *kvi*, fold, pen.
>
> (*Dictionary of Old Icelandic*, 1910)

There is also the problem of trying to work out the original
name from the various modifications it has gone through
at the hands of speakers of a different language. An example
is the Norse name Guirdil in Gaelic-speaking Rum. We
have a pre-Clearance spelling by courtesy of Mr Clarke
who was obviously trying to get at the correct form.

> We landed near a farm, called Guidhl, or Gewdale, or as it
> is in Mackenzie's chart, Guaridil.
>
> (Edward Daniel Clarke, 1797)

Despite the absence of 'habitative' names there are certain
place-names which have extra significance. Compounds
such as Smeordail (butter-dale, Eigg), where both

elements are Norse, are particularly persuasive. Rangail in Rum may include as its suffix the Norse element -*vollr* or field, which can only have been given by a Norse farmer. *Tobhta* comes from a Norse word *topt* which also occurs in English as toft. It was used formerly as a settlement term and occurs a number of times in islands such as Skye, Coll and Mull. We also find it in Eigg and Canna:

> It was over on the brae of Kildonan that he was living, a place we call to this day *Tobhta Dhughaill*.
>
> (Mackinnon, *Tocher 10*, 1973)

Arguments about what place-names prove can never really be settled. The nature and density of Norse names in the Small Isles, even a thousand years after they were first given, indicate Norse political control. Most of the principal farms in Eigg have Norse names. What we can never know are the proportions of the social mix. How many Picts or Gaels survived? Perhaps the likeliest scenario is that Norse colonists dominated the upper sections of local society and renamed most of the principal farms and settlement sites. The Gaels or Picts survived lower down the social scale, which is why some demonstrably pre-Norse names such as Kildonnan and Kilmory have persisted. Kil-names did not become Kirk-names. We do not find Kirkaboll or Kirkibost as in Tiree or Skye. If the Gaelic population of the Small Isles had been wiped out then why do we still find dedications to these early saints?

The problem is illustrated by the islanders themselves:

> The language, principally spoken, and universally understood, is Gaelic, and from it the names of places seem mostly to be derived; yet it must be confessed, that there are names of places, which the present inhabitants do not fully understand, that seem to be derived from a

language or languages to them unknown; but supposed to be Danish.

(M'Lean *Old Statistical Account,*
Parish of Small Isles, 1794)

In other words the islanders looked for the meaning or significance of the names they used, as people have always done, and sometimes could not find a Gaelic explanation.

Land-assessment

There is a unique land-assessment system that has long been associated with the Norse colonies in Scotland. This is in terms of two units, ouncelands and pennylands, which may or may not have a common origin. These units are found throughout the Highlands and Islands as well as the Northern Isles, the northern mainland and south-west Scotland. There is considerable debate as to the origin and development of this system, or systems, and the variety of functions it may have served, for example military levy and civil or religious taxation. For the purposes of this chapter I am only going to deal with the evidence that refers directly to the Small Isles.

Ouncelands are large units, suitable for big land grants. Smaller units were needed to define the individual holdings. These are provided by pennylands and their further subdivision into half-pennies, farthings and so on. In the Western Isles and along the west coast, ouncelands were subdivided into twenty pennylands, whereas in the far north an ounceland was eighteen pennylands. The reason for the twenty pennyland rate may have been that it fitted neatly on top of a previous Dalriadic/Pictish system of a davach divided into twenty houses. The pennyland assessment became the basis for the whole rural economy until the eighteenth century.

We are fortunate to have two early charters for Eigg that allow us to work out the complete assessment for the island. All that remains uncertain is what conclusions we should draw as to the origin and purpose of this system. It is a valuation on the basis of productivity, not area; some areas were accorded higher values than others.

In 1498 James IV gave two charters for the island which are recorded in the Register of the Great Seal. He granted about two-thirds of the island to Clanranald, and the other third to the family of Macdonald of Morar. Since we know that an ounceland consisted of twenty pennylands throughout the Hebrides we can deduce that Eigg originally consisted of five ouncelands. Several of the settlements are split in the charters but if we recompose them as in Figure 2 and Map 6 we come closer to an original valuation which possibly represents the earliest Viking pattern of settlement and land allocation. It seems that ouncelands still provided the underlying definitions even as late as 1498. The division of the island into two sections of twenty-one merklands and nine merklands does not make arithmetical sense. However these are equivalent to divisions of 3.5 ouncelands and 1.5 ouncelands which is much more logical.

Can we map the division into ouncelands more precisely? We are fortunate that two estate maps for Eigg have survived. In 1806 William Bald drew a map of the island and Thompson another in 1824 which was based on Bald's. These add to our knowledge by displaying the farm boundaries. Now while these can change over time in many parts of the Highlands they have not done so in practice, not least because boundaries are so often set by geography and natural features.

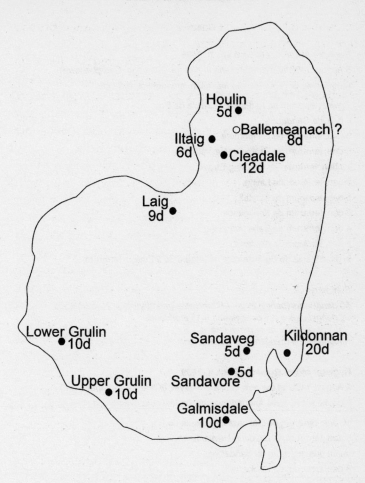

Map 6   The Norse valuation of Eigg

The Small Isles

Register of the Great Seal vol. II, 2438

5 August 1498 'at the new castle in Kintyre' (Kilkerran, Campbeltown)

King James IV gives Ranald Makallan, amongst other lands,

6 merc. terrarum de Kildonen, in insula de Eg;

4 den. de Sandabeg,

5 den. terrarum de Sandamore,

5 den. terrarum de Grudleng-Neyvaidlean,

10 den. terrarum de Grudling-Etrach,

9 den. terrarum de Layng,

5 den. terrarum de Claytall,

3 den. terrarum de Knokeltnok,

4 den. terrarum de Ballemeanach,

5 den. terrarum de Houland,

in dicta insula de Eg, extenden. in integro ad 21 merc. terrarum;

Summary:

50 denariatas (pennylands) + 6 mercatas (merklands) = 21 merklands
50 pennylands = 2.5 ouncelands = 15 merklands
Ratio of ouncelands to merklands = 1:6
Kildonnan = 6 merklands or 1 ounceland

Register of the Great Seal vol. II, 2439

5 August 1498 'at the new castle in Kintyre' (Kilkerran, Campbeltown)

King James IV gives Angus Rewochsoun Makranald, amongst other lands,

10 den. terrarum de Galmastal, in insula de Eg;

5 den. terrarum de Grudling-Neyvaidlean,

unam den. terrarum de Sandabeg,

3 den. terrarum de Knokelturk,

7 den. terrarum de Claytall

4 den. terrarum de Ballemeanach,

in insula de Eg, extenden. in integro ad 9 merc. terrarum;

Summary:
30 denariatas (pennylands) = 9 merklands
30 pennylands = 1.5 ouncelands = 9 merklands
Ratio of ouncelands to merklands = 1:6

Ouncelands?

If we collate the two charters of 1498 we arrive at the following

10d	Galmisdale
10d	Grulin-Neyvaidlean
10d	Grulin-Etrach
5d	Sandaveg
5d	Sandamore
9d	Laig
12d	Cleadale
8d	Ballemeanach
5d	Houlin
6d	Knokelturk
6m or 20d	Kildonnan

Total valuation of Eigg = 30 merklands or 100 pennylands or 5 ouncelands

If we refine this list further we can surmise the original division into 5 ouncelands:

20d	Grulin
20d	Galmisdale & Sanda
20d	Kildonnan
20d	Cleadale & Ballemeanach?
20d	Laig, Houlin & Knokelturk?

Of these names:

Norse	Galmisdale, Sanda, Cleadale, Laig
Norse?	Grulin, Howlin
Gaelic/Norse?	Knokelturk (Cnoc Iltaig)
Gaelic	Kildonnan, Ballemeanach

Figure 2   Eigg charters

If we superimpose the farm-boundaries of 1824 on to our notional Norse ouncelands we end up with a projection of those ouncelands as in Map 7. A presumption of continuity is reinforced by the fact that many later rentals, tacks and wadsets refer to the pennyland valuations of the land concerned. These can only have had continued meaning if the boundaries remained intact. Although they started off life as valuations, over the centuries particular pennylands became associated with specific areas of land.

What is intriguing is that the principal Norse farm, the most valuable farm on the island and the probable home of the local Norse chief, retained its pre-Norse name of Kildonnan. If, as suggested in the previous chapter, this davach or ounceland was originally the endowment of a Dalriadic monastery then the unit was previously Dalriadic or Pictish. The Norse simply adopted the existing farm, its name, its value and therefore its boundaries.

The pennyland system is the key to the structure of the Highland rural economy. Of course, there were variations in practice from one place to another, and modifications as the Highlands came into contact with the Lowlands. In some areas the pennyland was replaced by the merkland, a Scottish land-assessment unit. In the Small Isles the pennyland system formed the basis for the allocation of land and possibly other resources such as sea-weed and sea-birds. It underlay civil and religious taxation, and military levy. It was the basis for souming arrangements and rural policing. It probably underwrote payments to local officials. Certain functions may have accrued over time but others are likely to have been undertaken from the very beginning.

There is evidence from many parts of the Highlands and Hebrides that the pennyland system was still active in the eighteenth century. David Bruce's rentals of the

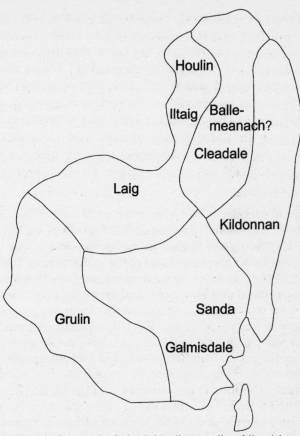

There is an element of doubt in the north of the island. Ballemeanach has disappeared and a new unit called Five Pennies has come into existence.

Map 7   Eigg's ouncelands?

Small Isles bring this out. In Kirktoun of Canna the small tenants all paid rent at the flat rate of £20 Scots (30 merks) per pennyland; or fractions thereof if they held smaller units, that is £10 for a half-pennyland, £15 for a three-quarter pennyland and so on. The greater tenants who held the 'toun and lands' of Tarbert, or Coroghon and Sanday, seem to have paid at a lower rate of 20 merks per pennyland. In addition clan officers were rewarded in terms of the pennyland assessment. So for instance the 'Ground Officer' was effectively given a half-pennyland for his trouble.

> Donald McIsaac in Kirktoun in the said Island of Canna Who being Solemnly Sworn and Interrogat Deposes That for Eighteen years bygone he has possessed without a written Tack One penny Land of the said Kirktoun That he took the possession thereof from the said Lady Dowager of Clanronald now Deceassed, And agreed to pay of yearly rent for the same, Twenty pounds Scotts in money one Sheep or one pound Scotts, But if demanded one pound four Shilling money forsaid And to releeve the Proprietor of the Kings Cess Ministers Stipend and haill other publick Burdens and Taxations And to perform Services when required Conform to use and wont . . . Deposes that he is allowed a yearly Deduction of one half of the above Rent for his being Ground Officer of the said Island of Canna

> (Kirktoun, Canna, 4 August 1748,
> David Bruce's Rental (E 744/1/2))

Thomas Pennant gives descriptions of the system in Canna and Rum just shortly before its demise. He writes of Canna:

> This was the property of the bishop of the isles, but at present that of Mr MacDonald of Clan-Ronald. His factor, a resident agent, rents most of the island, paying two guineas for each penny-land; and these he sets to the poor

people at four guineas and a half each; and exacts, besides this, three days labor in the quarter from each person. Another head tenant possesses other penny-lands, which he sets in the same manner, to the impoverishing and very starving of the wretched inhabitants.

The penny-lands derive their name from some old valuation. The sum requisite to stock one is thirty pounds: it maintains seven cows and two horses: and the tenant can raise on it eight bolls of small black oats, the produce of two; and four of bear from half a boll of seed; one boll of potatoes yields seven. The two last are manured with sea-tang.

The arable land in every farm is divided into four parts, and lots are cast for them at Christmas: the produce, when reaped and dried, is divided among them in proportion to their rents; and for want of mills is ground in the quern. All the pasture is common, from May to the beginning of September.

And of Rum:

Here is an absurd custom of allotting a certain stock to the land; for example, a farmer is allowed to keep fourteen head of cattle, thirty sheep, and six mares, on a certain tract called a penny-land. (The division into penny-lands, and much of the rural oeconomy agree in both islands.) The person who keeps more is obliged to repair out of his superfluity any loss his neighbour may sustain in his herds or flocks. . . .

Every penny-land is restricted to twenty-eight sums of cattle: one milk cow is reckoned a sum, or ten sheep: a horse is reckoned two sums. By this regulation every person is at liberty to make up his sums with what species of cattle he pleases; but then is at the same time prevented from injuring his neighbor (in a place where grazing is in common) by rearing too great a stock. This rule is often broken; but by the former regulation, the sufferer may repair his loss from the herds of the avaritious.

No hay is made in this island, nor any sort of provender for winter provision. The domestic animals support themselves as well as they can on spots of grass preserved for that purpose. In every farm is one man, from his office called Fear cuartaich, whose sole business is to preserve the grass and corn: as a reward he is allowed grass for four cows, and the produce of as much arable land as one horse can till and harrow.

(Pennant *A Tour in Scotland and Voyage to the Hebrides*, 1772)

Pennant's evidence for the longevity of the pennyland system in Rum and Canna is supported by evidence for Eigg given by Hugh Mackinnon to the School of Scottish Studies.

Grulin . . . went with the farm of Laig too at that time. And there were fourteen families in Grulin at that time. There were, as we say, Lower Grulin and Upper Grulin . . . There were seven families in each village: that made fourteen families altogether.

And this is how the land was – how I heard the land was set out for them: anyway, my own grandfather was one of those who had a house there, and he and his brother shared a pennyland between them. And I used to ask my mother's brother what stock was the souming of a pennyland. He used to tell me that he heard from his father, that is, my grandfather, my own grandfather, that it was five cows and one horse that was the souming of a pennyland.

(Hugh Mackinnon talking of Grulin in 1853, *Tocher 10*, 1973)

Hugh Mackinnon's evidence differs from Pennant's, which is itself inconsistent, with regard to the stocking levels allowed on a pennyland. It certainly seems to have varied from one area to another depending on local circumstances.

The only trace we find of this system in Rum is the place-name An Leth-Pheighinn (the half-pennyland) at

the junction between the Kilmory and Kinloch river systems. For much of the mediaeval period two townships are mentioned in Rum, Harris worth 2 merks and Kilmory worth 4 merks. Unfortunately it is not possible to translate these exactly into pennylands (of which there were twenty in Rum) but no doubt the little hamlets marked on Langlands' Map of Argyll were reckoned at assessments of a farthing or more.

Map 8 shows the overall ounceland assessment system in the Small Isles. In terms of land-value Eigg was worth more than the other three islands put together. Our earliest population figures, based on Skene's anonymous sixteenth-century source, suggest that the distribution of population matched this. The early assessors were very pragmatic people. Muck, the smallest isle, has the same value as Rum, the largest.

Personal names

Personal names also indicate a Norse presence in the Hebrides. Some, such as Torquil or MacAskill, are demonstrably Norse; however to do any sort of analysis we need lists of early inhabitants and these are scarce. Moreover, many names undergo metamorphosis as they are adapted to meet new cultural requirements. By the time they meet the light of day in a rental or census return they have often been transformed beyond recognition.

We do have a list of names in the Small Isles dating from 1765 which has recently been transcribed by Catherine MacInnes. Most of the names are typical of the Gaelic Highlands but there are one or two such as Unna McDonald from Eigg and Gatfery (Godfrey) McEdam in Canna whose names suggest a Norse heritage. Godred or Godfrey was common in the old Kingdom of

81

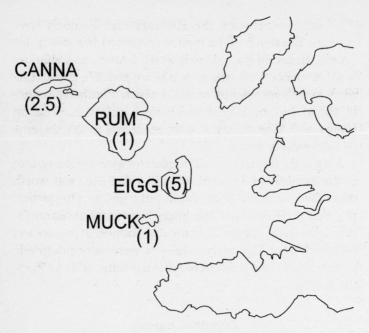

Map 8   Ouncelands in the Small Isles

Man. Unna, a name found frequently in Coll, may be the same as Aud, one of the earliest and most famous Viking women in the Hebrides.

Conclusions

Viking and Gael intermingled in proportions we cannot know. The islands may have been Norse-speaking or bilingual for some considerable period of time, otherwise it is difficult to see how Norse place-names would have stuck. However once the influx of new settlers dried up, so Gaelic eventually came to predominate. On the evidence of place-names the Norse presence is most marked in Canna, Eigg and Rum. It is less obvious in Muck.

On the basis of the population figures given at the end of the last chapter it seems unlikely that there were ever many families on Canna, Rum or Muck. It is understandable then that a relatively small number of Norse settlers would have a large impact in the Hebrides. We can envisage a situation in Canna where eight or ten Norse families had a similar number of Gaelic dependants. These Norse would marry among themselves and their neighbours in the islands in an effort to preserve their lands, their culture and their language. They may have done this successfully for a century or two. But all the while the tide of re-Gaelicisation was working north and west. This process of cultural conversion may have been relatively peaceful and, in the case of the northern Hebrides, incomplete before the Treaty of Perth.

4

The Mediaeval Period

THE SMALL ISLES BELONGED to the Norse from the first stages of Viking settlement *c.* 830 to the Treaty of Perth in 1266. We know little of the petty fiefdoms that operated in the early Norse period although we have some names, such as Ketil Flatnose and Earl Gilli of Coll, who may have exercised regional authority. From about 980–1065 the area fell under the sway of the Orkney Earls, Sigurd and Thorfinn. After the death of Thorfinn *c.* 1065 the focus of power shifted southwards and from 1079 the Kingdom of Man became the political authority in the area. In 1156 this kingdom was divided internally by the rebellion of the House of Somerled whose power-base lay in Argyll and the Southern Isles. From now on the southern Hebrides were controlled by the Macsorleys; the northern Hebrides, principally Skye and Lewis, by the Kings of Man, usually via a son or brother who was their local regent. We cannot be certain whether, at this stage, the Small Isles, Uist and Barra, were Macsorley lands or not. They certainly seem to have become so by the 1240s.

The Chronicles of Man describe the beginning of the process under Godred of Man *c.* 1155:

> When he saw that he was firmly established on the throne . . . he began exercising tyranny against his chieftains, . . . One of them . . . went to Somerled and requested from him his son Dougal, that he should make him king over the Isles. Somerled was very much pleased to hear this request and handed his son Dougal over to him, who took and conducted him through all the Isles. He subjected them all to his sway and received hostages from each island.
>
> (Broderick *Chronicles of the Kings of Man and the Isles*, 1979)

What is important about this statement is that, in the eyes of Hebrideans, Dougal had legitimacy whereas Somerled only had power. Dougal's mother, Raghnhildis, was daughter of the King of Man, and it was through their mother that Somerled's sons could claim a right to rule in the Isles. The Clanranald historian Macvurich confirms this. He claims that Dougal came to rule Argyll and Lorn while Ranald, another of Somerled's sons:

> went to the Hebrides and Kintyre, where his posterity succeeded him. . . . the rightful inheritance of the Isles came to Ranald, and his race after him, for the daughter of Olave the Red, son of Godfrey, was the mother of Ranald, son of Somerled. This daughter of Olave was the lawful heir of her father and of her two brothers, viz., Ranald and Olave the Black.
>
> (*Book of Clanranald* in Cameron (ed.) *Reliquiae Celticae*, Inverness, 1894)

This Ranald, son of Somerled, was the ancestor of both the Macruaris of Garmoran and the Macdonalds of Islay.

The branches reunited with the marriage of Amy, the last Macruari, to John of Islay in 1337.

Not only did the Kingdom of Man face internal division, it also faced external threats from a Scottish realm keen to extend its power over the Hebrides. Scottish pressure was felt in Bute and the Cumbraes before 1200. Geographically these were closest to the seat of Scots power and most susceptible. The Scots king mounted one, perhaps two, campaigns against southern Argyll in the 1220s. Possibly as a result of this the Macruaris were expelled or relocated their power-base to the Rough Bounds of Garmoran, the islands of Eigg, Rum and Uist. It is difficult to know exactly how and when this estate took shape; Ranald may simply have inherited it after Somerled's death in 1164 or it may have grown by acquisition. Garmoran may have come from Somerled, but the islands must have come through Ragnhildis, Somerled's wife.

Norse or Scot?

In 1248, according to *Hakon Hakon's Son's saga*, Dugald Macruari was in Bergen with his cousin, John Macdougall of Argyll. Both pleaded with King Hakon for the title of king over the Northern Hebrides. In this instance John was successful and Dugald was disappointed. However there are several later saga references to Dugald being a king, so at some stage he may have replaced John or been given a compensatory title. Although John of Argyll demonstrated his loyalty to Hakon in 1249 he had switched loyalties to Scotland by 1263. Dugald's apparent elevation may have had something to do with this. It would have been politically sensible for Hakon to maintain a rivalry between these two branches of the Macsorleys under the old maxim of divide and rule.

1a and 1b. Canna, A' Chill: Canna 1, face and drawing (RCAHMS)

2a and 2b. Canna, A' Chill: Canna 1, reverse and drawing (RCAHMS)

3a. Waldenbuch, sculptured stone (Württembergisches Landesmuseum, Stuttgart); 3b and 3c. Canna 2, both faces (RCAHMS)

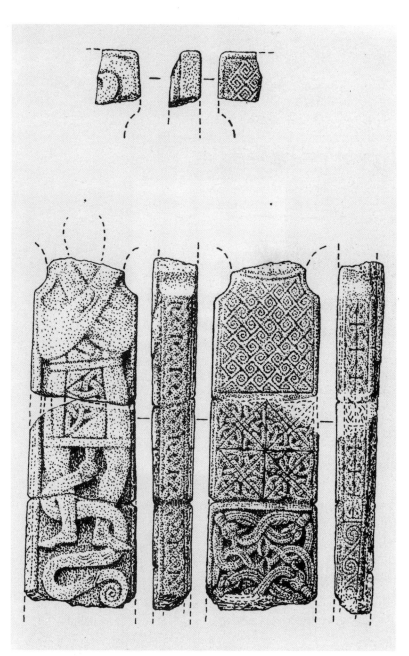

4. Canna 2, drawing (RCAHMS)

Rum

Canna

Canna

Canna

Eigg

Rum

Muck

Eigg

Eigg

5. Early Christian stones in the Small Isles (D. Rixson)

Cruciform stone (Rum)

Detail from Cross (Canna)

Cross-slab(s)? (Eigg)

Detail from cross-slab (Canna)

Cross-slab (Eigg)

6. Early Christian stones in the Small Isles (D. Rixson)

7a. St Clement's Church, Rodel, Harris: detail of Macleod tomb, showing a hunting scene, AD 1528 (RCAHMS)

7b. Kilmory, Knapdale: MacMillan cross, detail of hunting scene (RCAHMS)

8. Rum: possible deer trap (RCAHMS)

9. Coroghon Castle, Canna (D. Rixson)

10. Rum from Eigg (D. Rixson)

In 1249 Alexander II of Scotland mounted a naval expedition to the west coast, and although he died prematurely at Kerrera, Scottish intent was clear. They wished to reclaim the Hebrides, by force if necessary. The Macsorleys were in a difficult position since they held their mainland estates from the King of Scotland but their islands from the King of Norway. This dilemma could only be resolved by a political choice, which was partly decided by military pressure. Some time after 1249 John (Macdougall) shifted his allegiance to Scotland while Dugald (Macruari) remained with Norway. He may have felt the Norse would help him regain the territories he had lost in south Argyll. Or it may be that, like the Macdonalds of Islay, his own political stance was defined by rivalry with, and opposition to, the Macdougalls of Lorn.

In 1253 Hakon levied men for a campaign against Denmark in which both John and Dugald participated. Contact between the Norwegian court and the Hebrides seems to have been well maintained: in the summer of 1262 letters were sent from the Hebrides to Norway complaining of Scots aggression, particularly in Skye. That winter Hakon prepared for an invasion the following year. In the spring of 1263 messengers were sent to Dugald telling him to expect a Norwegian fleet in the summer. Dugald used the news to good effect and spread the rumour that forty ships were coming. This deterred any further Scots aggression. It appears that Dugald acted as the principal Norwegian agent in the Hebrides.

In the 1263 expedition Eric, son of Dugald, was on board Hakon's enormous flagship. Eric is a Norwegian name and this raises the possibility that his mother was Norwegian, perhaps even a lesser member of Hakon's family. It would be entirely in keeping for Hakon to seek to bind these independent Hebrideans closer to him by marital ties as well as military obligations. After all, in 1248 he had given his daughter Cecilia in marriage to King Harold of Man.

It is clear from *Hakon Hakon's Son's saga*, that Dugald was one of Hakon's principal supporters, unlike the other two branches of MacSorleys. In 1263 John of Argyll refused point-blank to help Hakon and told him he would rather forego his Hebridean dominions than lose his even larger estates in mainland Scotland. John could suffer at the hands of Hakon's fleet but, if the worst came to the worst, his people could always retreat inland. The chiefs of Islay and Kintyre did not have this option and were persuaded by *force majeure*. Hakon's fleet consisted of between 100 and 200 ships and there was nothing the islanders could do but accept Hakon's terms. Dugald's men apparently acted as intermediaries in these negotiations so we can assume that some at least of the Macruaris were bilingual. Dugald's brother Alan was extremely active against the Scots, raiding far and wide after part of Hakon's fleet was portaged from Loch Long over to Loch Lomond.

After the stand-off at Largs, Hakon's fleet sailed back northwards. When he got to Mull, Hakon parted from Dugald and Alan Macruari. He gave John of Argyll's island possessions to Dugald as well as what was probably Dunaverty Castle in Kintyre. He then sailed north to an island which has sometimes been translated Rum, sometimes Rona. Given that it was en route from Mull to Skye the former seems more likely. In the original the name is written *Raun-eyja* and *Raun-eyjum*. It may be relevant that Dean Monro, who, in 1549 wrote one of the earliest topographical descriptions of Rum, calls it Ronin.

King Hakon sickened and died in Kirkwall. With him ended Norwegian attempts to retain the Hebrides. Eric, son of Dugald, must have returned to Norway after 1263 because in 1264 the new king, Magnus, sent him back to the Hebrides in a well-manned, 36-oar ship. However the Orcadians were so concerned about a potential Scottish raid that the newly appointed Norse commander, Ogmund Crow-dance, kept Eric with him in Orkney over the winter of 1264–5. In 1264 the Scots forced Angus of Islay and Magnus of Man to come to terms but, as *Magnus Hakon's Son's saga* says:

> Lord Dugald defended himself in ships, and they took no hold of him.

(Anderson, *Early Sources*)

Dugald also had mainland possessions in Garmoran (Knoydart, Morar, Arisaig and Moidart), and he used his land-forces to good effect. In 1264 the Scots had exacted much tribute from Caithness but Dugald intervened, purloined the treasure and slew the lawman of the Scots. In the spring of 1265 Dugald came to Orkney asking for men. With him were his son Eric and two others who were probably Orcadians. Between them they had three ships but it was all in vain. The Scots were geographically close and could exert continuous military pressure. The Norwegians had no inclination to fight expensive campaigns in order to retain fractious islands of dubious worth. Intermediaries went back and forth and negotiations culminated in the Treaty of Perth in 1266. By this the Hebrides were ceded to the Scots in return for a yearly payment. Dugald had now to make an accommodation with his new master. This can hardly have been a prospect he relished. The damage he and his brother had caused in 1263 and 1264 would still be fresh in Scottish memory.

There are two clauses in the Treaty of Perth which suggest that the negotiators had the Macruari predicament in mind. Islanders were pardoned for damages done to the Scots and granted freedom to leave if they wished. While emigration was not a practical option except for the very wealthy, the inclusion of such conditions suggests that the Norwegian negotiators were not just engaged in a paper exercise. Such clauses were designed to protect pro-Norse families like the Macruaris, families which had been prepared to fight to retain Norse sovereignty over the Hebrides.

> All the men of the said islands which are ceded, resigned and quit-claimed to the said lord king of Scots . . . shall be subject to the laws and customs of the realm of Scotland and be judged and dealt with according to them henceforth, but for the misdeeds or injuries and damage which they have committed hitherto while they adhered to the said king of Norway they be no wise punished or molested in their heritages in those islands but stand peacefully therein under the lordship of the king of Scots . . . if they should wish to remain in the said islands under the lordship of the said lord king of Scots, they may remain in his lordship freely and in peace, but if they wish to retire they may do so, with their goods, lawfully, freely and in full peace; so that they be not compelled either to remain or to retire
>
> (Donaldson *Scottish Historical Documents*, 1970)

Our sources for these events are principally the Norse sagas, in particular that of *Hakon Hakon's Son*. Saga material is not always credited with much historical value but in this case we know the saga was composed very shortly after the events which it describes and so they were fresh in the minds of participants. Unfortunately, after this our Norwegian sources run dry and our Scottish sources are sparse.

In the first volume of the *Acts of Parliament of Scotland* there is a paragraph listing a number of documents then extant (1282), which concerned Norway. They included letters and charters touching on the erstwhile Norse possessions in Scotland and matters of mutual interest such as shipwreck. Some of these documents were written in Norwegian. Places referred to include Man, Bute, Caithness and Orkney. One short sentence runs:

> A letter of the King of Norway about the lands of Uist and Eigg.

Unfortunately we have no further information but given the troubled Macruari relationship with Scotland and the details of the Treaty of Perth it seems likely that there was some dispute with their new masters. The Macruaris owned both Uist and Eigg and had presumably appealed to the King of Norway to intercede on their behalf. The letter did not cover all the Macruari estates. It did not touch on Garmoran because that had always been Scottish. It only dealt with the island domains which had recently seen a change in sovereignty.

The phrase 'about the lands of Uist and Eigg' suggests a general issue rather than something specific. Whatever it was affected these islands but not the mainland estates of Garmoran. Uist at this time almost certainly meant the whole of the southern half of the Long Island, that is, North Uist to Barra, and included St Kilda. Eigg was far more important than Rum, the only other Macruari possession in the Small Isles. Effectively the phrase 'Uist and Eigg' meant the Macruari island possessions. One issue that would certainly concern the Macruaris was how much the Scottish king was going to tax them on these lands.

Taxation from Bergen may not have been unduly heavy before 1266 but the new authority was much closer to hand. Our only clue as to the relative weight of Scottish taxation is the conversion rate that obtained between the two assessment systems, ouncelands (Norse) and merklands

(Scottish). This ratio varied through the Highlands and Hebrides. It was as high as 1 ounceland to 10 merklands in Kintyre, through 1:6 in the Small Isles, 1:4 in much of Skye, to 1:1 in Knoydart (Garmoran).

It may be that what was in dispute was the exchange rate imposed on the Macruari estates in Uist and the Small Isles. Perhaps the Scots assessors thought they were worth more than other parts of the northern Hebrides, which may well have been the case, or they may have felt it was payback time for Dugald's interception of the taxes from Caithness. It was nevertheless an important issue. In those days a land-assessment or 'extent' served exactly the same purpose as a rating valuation does today. The Norwegian king may have been appealing a heavy property revaluation on behalf of an erstwhile supporter.

In 1292 King John Balliol instituted three sheriffdoms on the west coast. The lands within each sheriffdom are listed and while the text is not fully preserved the outlines are clear. The Sheriffdom of Skye included Ross, Glene[lg?], Skye and Lewis, eight davachs of what was probably Garmoran (in other words, Moidart, Arisaig, Morar and Knoydart), Eigg, Rum, Uist and Barra with their small islands. The Sheriffdom of Lorn covered most of Argyll from Ardnamurchan and Morvern southwards while the Sheriffdom of Kintyre included south Argyll, Kintyre and Bute.

The Sheriffdom of Skye, therefore, included the whole of the Macruari estate. Moreover this estate is described in the same way (Garmoran, Eigg, Rum, Uist and Barra) in four charters in the fourteenth century. At the end of the Norse period there was an extremely pro-Norse family of Macruaris who owned the two largest Small Isles as well as the mainland to the east and the islands of Barra and Uist to the west. The fact that this estate is coupled with lands further north which had previously belonged

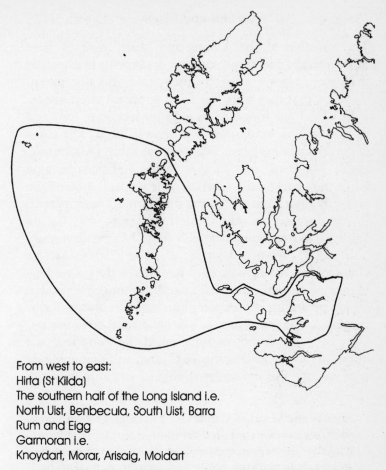

From west to east:
Hirta (St Kilda)
The southern half of the Long Island i.e.
North Uist, Benbecula, South Uist, Barra
Rum and Eigg
Garmoran i.e.
Knoydart, Morar, Arisaig, Moidart

Map 9　The Macruari estate in the early fourteenth century

to the King of Man (Glenelg, Lewis and Skye) suggests
that perhaps Dugald Macruari had in fact been king over
the Northern Hebrides at some stage after 1249. For a
short period in the thirteenth century the islands of Eigg
and Rum lay at the heart of an estate belonging to a family
of enormous power (see Map 9).

Canna and Muck

The omission of both Canna and Muck from all these thirteenth and fourteenth century documents implies that they were always church lands; that did not mean, however, that they were free from temporal interference.

In 1203 Pope Innocent issued a protection to Iona and its possessions, among which Canna is listed. The tenor of the document suggests that Iona was subject to temporal abuse. We know that Vikings in the Hebrides became Christian early and Christian sculptural patronage certainly flourished on Canna during the Viking period. It therefore seems reasonable to suppose that Canna belonged to Iona uninterruptedly from the seventh century until 1203. However laymen, whether Viking, Gael or Gall-Gaidhil, have always been tempted by the possessions of the church, while the ecclesiastical authorities depended on lay power for protection. This was not always forthcoming, as the complaints of 1203 and 1428 demonstrate.

In 1428 the Abbot of Iona asked the Pope to grant immunity to the inhabitants of Canna, and that anybody who violated this immunity should be excommunicated. His reasons were:

> Since in the island of Canna ... by reason of wars and other calamities in the past divers homicides, depredations and other ills were perpetrated, so that some strong men of the familiars of the Abbot and convent were slain by pirates and sea rovers, and divers farmers and inhabitants of the island were afraid to reside there and cultivate the land, and transferred themselves elsewhere, deserting the island to the no little loss of the said monastery

> (Scottish History Society *Calendar of Scottish Supplications to Rome*, 1956)

So despite belonging to Iona it seems that the island of

Canna was subject to some disturbance. We come across both Canna and Muck in a Rental of the Bishopric of the Isles and Abbey of Iona which was drawn up in 1561.

> The Abbatis landis within the Clanrannaldis boundis
> Item, the Ile of Cannay . . .

> Rentale of Bischopis landis within the Illis . . .
> Item, the Ille callit Ellanamwk, possest be M'Aen of Ardnamurchane

> (*Collectanea de Rebus Albanicis*, 1847)

With the marriage of Amy Macruari to John of Islay in 1337 the Macruari dynasty ended. Their estates were increasingly fragmented although a core passed down to the Clanranald family. However, Macruari wealth and power in the thirteenth and fourteenth centuries helps explain two mysterious aspects of the Small Isles: the crosses of Eigg and the deer-traps of Rum.

The Eigg Crosses

After marrying Amy Macruari for her lands John of Islay later put her away in order to marry Margaret Stewart, daughter of Robert II. On his death John's children by Margaret were preferred for the Lordship of the Isles. His children by Amy retained the old Macruari estate.

> Ranald, the son of John, was High Steward over the Isles at the time of his father's death, being in advanced age and ruling over them. On the death of his father he called a meeting of the nobles of the Isles and of his brethren at one place, and he gave the sceptre to his brother at Cill Donan in Eigg, and he was nominated Macdonald and Donald of Isla, contrary to the opinion of the men of the Isles. A man of augmenting churches and monasteries was this Ranald, son of John, son of Angus Og, from whom the

name of Clann Ranald has been applied to this race . . . He was governor of the whole of the Northern Coastland and of the Isles, until he died in the year of the age of Christ 1386, in his own manor of Castle Tirim, having left a family of five sons.

(Macvurich *Book of Clanranald* in
Reliquiae Celticae, vol. II, 1894)

Hugh Macdonald of Sleat confirms this in the seventeenth century:

Ranald . . . gave over the tutory to Donald, his brother, in Egg.

(*Collectanea de Rebus Albanicis,* 1847)

Several facts emerge from this evidence. Eigg was a focal point in the Macruari/Clanranald estate. The island chiefs felt Ranald should not have given precedence to his half-brother, despite Donald's royal blood. Ranald was governor of the Northern Hebrides and adjacent mainland, which sounds like the kingship exercised by Dugald Macruari over a century earlier. Ranald was a patron of the church.

Now the 1428 plea to Rome clearly states that Canna lay in the parish of Kildonnan, a parish that was probably instituted by the Macruaris. However, the parish church of Kildonnan does not contain any of the mediaeval grave-slabs which are so common elsewhere in the Highlands and Islands. With the exception of a rather unusual and probably late slab from Canna they are conspicuous by their absence. It seems that Kildonnan was not the preferred burial-ground of either the Macruaris or the Clanranalds. Instead we find them in Uist, Kilmory (Arisaig) or Eilean Fhianain (Loch Shiel, Moidart). What we do find in Eigg are a series of stone crosses. There were at least four of these, which is quite remarkable for an island this size. Known sites include Druim na Croise (near Howlin), Glac an Dorchadais in the middle of the island (NM 47988642), Crois Mhor (Kildonnan) and Crois Moraig (Grulin).

There is a tradition that these crosses were deliberately sited to be in view of each other. Hugh Miller writes:

> On the edge of an eminence, on which the traveller journeying westwards catches the last glimpse of the chapel of St Donan, there had once been a rude cross erected, and another rude cross on an eminence on which he catches the last glimpse of the first; and that there had thus been a chain of stations formed from sea to sea, . . . till, last of all, the emphatically holy point of the island, – the burial-place of the old Culdee, – came full in view.

(Miller *The Cruise of the Betsey,* 1845)

Who commissioned them? In Kildonnan there are the shaft and head of what are thought to be two crosses. The interlaced foliage on the cross-shaft is strikingly similar to that on the Campbeltown Cross which has been dated to about 1380. The cross-head has similar foliage and the shape of the disc-head also closely matches that of Campbeltown. The date fits well with the lifetime of Ranald, founder of the Clanranald, who died in the late 1380s. He had sufficient power and wealth to commission such major works of art and we know he patronised the church. The Macruaris may have chosen not to be buried in Kildonnan but they favoured Eigg in other ways.

Sheela-na-gig?

There is one other carving in Eigg which should be mentioned here. There is a slab from Kildonnan which, although now badly eroded, is thought to have been a sheela-na-gig. What were sheela-na-gigs?

They are carvings, often found in churches, which consist of a female displaying, or drawing attention to, her genitals. Given the subject-matter it is perhaps not surprising that they have been little discussed. Nevertheless whilst they may cause offence to some we should recognise them as part of our scant material heritage.

There have been two separate approaches to the subject. One has been to view them as female fertility figures which Christianity had somehow to accommodate. Like healing wells the church had to absorb whatever challenge or threat such carvings offered to the Christian belief system. Now there is no doubt that some dubious pagan practices survived in the mediaeval church in the Highlands; we have the evidence of Martin Martin and references to bull-sacrifice in Applecross. We also have a cross-slab from Rona which clearly depicts a set of male genitals. However such pagan hangovers tend to be particular and local whereas sheelas are found throughout the British Isles and in Ireland, France and Spain.

A second approach has been to view them as part of the mediaeval church's iconographic armoury. That they were depictions, often brutally ugly, of moral dilemmas; that they were used to promote rather than usurp the church's moral propositions; that by portraying sexuality in this way the church was teaching. In favour of this is the simple fact that so many sheelas have a religious context. They often appear as part of the fabric of the church. Such carvings seem to have flourished in the twelfth century and it is easy to see that fashions in France, Spain, Britain and Ireland could have influenced the Hebrides.

Unfortunately we have too few sheelas in the Highlands to draw any but the most general conclusions. They survive, though badly worn, in Rodel, Iona, Muckairn, Kilvickeon (Mull), Killevin (Argyll) and Eigg. We also know of one that used to be in Kilmartin which was known as *Iomaigh na Leasg* (The Image of Laziness). Such a name lends support to the theory of moral teaching. If these carvings date back to the twelfth century then their current positions in church walls and other places simply means they were rescued from earlier buildings and incorporated in later. The Eigg sheela may come from the first parish church at Kildonnan, perhaps built by an early Macruari.

Rum: A hunting reserve?

If Eigg was a political and religious focus for the Macruari and Clanranald dynasty then Rum was their playground. In the early mediaeval period Rum still belonged to Clanranald rather than Maclean. There is evidence that Rum was maintained as a hunting-reserve by the early mediaeval chiefs.

Muck and Canna were certainly, Eigg probably, too small to have supported any numbers of deer alongside a significant human presence. The deer population would always be under threat. Rum though, is different. It is substantially the largest of the Small Isles and a far lower percentage of its land is suitable for cultivation. Moreover there is evidence that hunting deer in Rum was long-lasting and formalised. Our evidence is of two types, written and material.

There is plenty of documentary evidence for the great Anglo-Norman royal forests but we know less about their Dark Age predecessors. Scots, Picts and Norse all hunted and, at one time or other, all dominated the west coast. Their hunting traditions are largely hidden from us except through carved stones or poetry. However there is no reason to assume that the institution of game reserves only started in the mediaeval period. We shall never know the contributions of Picts or Norse to hunting practice in the west, but once the area came under the sway of the Scottish realm we begin to get written accounts. Fordun establishes a connection between the number of inhabitants and the quality of the sport.

> Little Cumbrae, renowned for sport, but thinly inhabited.
> . . .
>
> Dura, twenty-four miles long, with few inhabitants, but affording very good sport . . .
>
> Rum . . . with excellent sport, but few inhabitants.
>
> (John of Fordun *Chronicle of the Scottish Nation, c.* 1380)

The similarity of phrasing raises the question of whether all these islands were deliberately maintained as waste or uncultivated lands. Were these the Gaelic equivalents of the great Anglo-Norman forests, or were they older still? A late sixteenth-century description, given by Skene, tells us how many fighting men each island could muster.

> Eg . . . will raise 60 men to the weiris. . . .
> Romb is ane Ile of small profit, except that it conteins mony deir, and for sustentation thairof the same is permittit unlabourit, except twa townis. It is . . . all hillis and waist glennis, and commodious only for hunting of deir. . . . and will raise 6 or 7 men. . . .
> Canna . . . will raise 20 men. . . .
> Ellan na Muk . . . will raise to the weiris 16 able men.
>
> (Skene *The Description of the Isles of Scotland,* 1577–95)

In later times Rum maintained a relatively large population.

It appears from Skene that, at the end of the sixteenth century, it was kept sparsely populated in order to maintain high numbers of deer. This is confirmed by Cornelius Ward, a Franciscan missionary, who noted in 1625 that there were only three villages in Rum.

How were these deer hunted?

We have various bits of evidence. On Rum itself there are some stone structures which have always been associated with deer-hunts. We have documentary evidence, some of which relates to Rum, and some of which allows us to draw analogies with other parts of Scotland. We have some place-names which suggest hunting.

Unfortunately it is difficult to interpret ruinous stone structures which, by their very nature, were roughly built and only for occasional use. Equally the vocabulary used in the documentary sources can be confusing, not least because these sources cover wide areas of space and time. The fact that authors were sometimes writing about practices that had long since vanished, and which they didn't fully understand, only compounds the problem.

In the context of Rum there are two technical terms which occur in the records. The first is *timchioll* (Gaelic) which tends to be anglicised to *tainchell*, *tynchell* and so on. It describes the circuit of beaters who drove the deer towards the waiting huntsmen. Secondly there were seats or *saitts* which refer to the positions adopted by the huntsmen as they waited for the deer. These seem to have been concealed so that the animals would not take fright until it was too late. There is a third term, *elerig*, which we do not find in documents about Rum but which almost certainly describes the type of trap used in the island. An *elerig* or *eileag* was a type of stone bag-net. The deer were funnelled into a high-sided stone enclosure which entrapped them.

> RONIN. . . . ane forest of heigh mountains, and abundance of litle deire in it, quhilk deir will never be slane dounewithe, but the principal saitts man be in the height of the hill, because the deir will be callit upwart, ay be the Tainchell, or without tynchell they will pass upwart perforce. . . .

> DURAY . . . ane ather fyne forrest for deire, . . . quhar is twa loches, meetand uthers throughe mide iyle, of salt water, to the lenthe of ane haff myle; and all the deire of the west pairt of that forrest, will be cahit be tainchess to that narrow entry, and the next day callit west againe, be tainchess through the said narrow entres, and infinit deire slaine there, pairt of small woods. This iyle, as the ancient iylanders alledges, should be callit Deiray, taking the name from the Deire in norne Leid, quhilk has given it that name in auld times.

> (Monro *A Description of the Western Isles of Scotland*, 1549)

Monro's description suggests a comparison between Rum and Jura, both because of the high deer population and the method of hunting. In both islands the deer were driven by the *timchioll* towards the huntsmen. In Rum the hunters waited for them in 'saitts' (seats). Jura, like Duirinish in Skye, has a name deriving from the Norse word for deer. Did the Norse give it this name because they *found* it full of deer, or because they *kept* it full of deer?

Monro's view of Jura is confirmed by Skene's source who says

> It is for the maist pairt wildernes and woodis, quhairin is mony deir, raes, and other wild beistis, quhairthrow thair is better hunting in this Ile nor ony of the rest.

> (Skene *The Description of the Isles of Scotland*, 1577–95)

and by Martin Martin a century later:

> JURA
> The hills ordinarily have about three hundred deer grazing
> on them, which are not to be hunted by any without the
> steward's licence.

(Martin *A Description of the Western
Islands of Scotland, c.* 1695)

Functions

Hunting was the sport of the nobility, enjoying high status
and a long history. This was expressed through the
literature and sculpture of the Highlands:

> One day Fionn, my lord, went to hunt . . . with three
> thousand nobles of the Fiana: they were unsurpassed in
> splendour . . .

> We carried war-raiment and arms whenever we so went
> hunting. I believe there was no warrior amongst them
> without a satin shirt and two hounds;

> Without a soft smooth wadded tunic . . . and his two spears
> in each man's hand . . .

> When Fionn had arranged our hounds, manifold to east
> and to west were the voices of dogs from hill to hill, starting
> boar and deer.

> Fionn himself and Bran were a while seated on the
> mountain. Every man of them was in his hunting position,
> till the deer's bristles rose.

> We loosed three thousand hounds who were both fierce
> and exceedingly active: every one of these killed two deer
> some time before the leashes were replaced in their collars.

> There fell six thousand horned deer in the valley beneath
> the mountain . . . such a hunt had never been before.

(Ross *Heroic Poetry from the Book of
the Dean of Lismore,* 1939)

This poem was written down *c*. 1500 and celebrates a fruitful hunt with dogs. There are any number of Pictish and mediaeval carved slabs which celebrate the chase. Hunting is a favourite motif in the mediaeval West Highland series. In Kilmory, Arisaig, there is a depiction of a huntsman armed with a bow. His dog, still leashed, pursues a stag and hind. As with aristocratic activities elsewhere no doubt there were elaborate conventions and a good deal of customary ritual. We have a cross-shaft from Kilmory, Knapdale, and a panel from Rodel, Harris, which portray striking costumes on the principal huntsmen (see Plate 7). The dogs from Kilmory seem to be of the mastiff type, those on the back of the Eigg cross-slab are more like greyhounds.

Picts, Scots and Scandinavians all regarded hunting as a noble activity. However it could also be turned into a spectacle and a major social event. This gave it wider cultural support and ensured that the necessary beaters participated. William Barclay, quoted by Pennant, writes of the year 1563:

> Two thousand Highlanders, or wild Scotch, as you call them here, were employed to drive to the hunting ground all the deer from the woods and hills of Atholo, Badenoch, Mar, Murray, and the countries about. As these Highlanders use a light dress, and are very swift of foot, they went up and down so nimbly that in less than two months' time they brought together 2,000 red deer, besides roes and fallow deer.

Hunting was also good training for war, and the hunters went well equipped:

> Now their weapons are long bowes and forked arrowes, swords and targets, harquebusses, muskets, durks and

Loquhabor-axes. With these armes I found many of them armed for hunting.

(Taylor 1618, quoted by Watson)

These military associations were extremely important in Highland culture. Rigour, hardiness, absence of comfort, are themes laboured by early Scots historians; surfeit and luxury are held responsible for the loss of past prowess. They enervate and make effete.

The drive

Taylor also describes how the drive was organised by the 'tinckhell':

The manner of the hunting is this – five or six hundred men do rise early in the morning, and they do disperse themselves divers ways, and seven, eight, or tenne miles compasse, they do bring in or chase in the deere in many herds, two, three, or four hundred in a herd, to such or such a place, as the noblemen shall appoint them. When the day is come the lords and gentlemen of their companys doe ride or goe to the said places . . . and then they being come to the place, do lye downe on the ground til those . . . scouts, which are called the tinckhell, doe bring down the deere . . . then after we had stayed three hours or thereabouts, we might perceive the deer appear on the hill round about us . . . which being followed by the tinckhell are chased down to the valley where we lay. Then all the valley on each side being waylaid with a hundred couple of strong Irish greyhounds, they are let loose as occasion serves upon the herd of deere, that with dogges, gunnes, arrowes, durkes, and daggers in the space of two houres four scores off fat deeres were slain.

(Taylor 1618, quoted by Watson)

Watson derives tinckhell from *timchioll*, a circuit and it is certainly this word that is used by Monro to describe hunting in Jura and Rum. These great drives usually took place in August, while the men were free before the harvest. By the eighteenth century hunting had switched to the modern method of stalking. A drive presupposes large numbers of people acting as beaters. A great chief could marshal such numbers in the mediaeval period, but not latterly.

In Taylor's example the *timchioll* drove the deer into the arms of the waiting huntsmen who would be stationed at 'seats'. An alternative, which was also used in Rum, was to drive them into an enclosure. This was known as an *elerig* or, in the far north and west, an *eileag*.

> While the deer were permitted to inhabit the valleys, and the country was under wood, the natives hunted them by surrounding them with men, or by making large enclosures of such a height as the deer could not overleap, fenced with stakes and intertwined with brushwood. Vast multitudes of men were collected on hunting days, who, forming a ring round the deer, drove them into these enclosures, which were open on one side. . . . The enclosures were called in the language of the country elerig.
>
> (Dr Robertson *Agriculture of the County of Perth*, 1799)

Decline

Chiefs were jealous of their reserves. They restricted access to those they wished and the law was a useful tool in the long-running feud between the newly powerful Clan Campbell and the old dynasty of Macdonald. In October 1633 criminal letters were issued at Inveraray against Ranald Macdonald of Benbecula, son of Allan of Clanranald. Among other accusations are the following:

> Item he and his servants and followers wherever he goes

'wears and bearis about with him hakbuttis gwnes and pistollis'.

Item contrary to the Acts of Parliament he is a common 'slayer of deare' and in the months of August and September 1632 he with a gun slew '6 deare in the Yle of Rowme' and also in July and August last [1633] with a gun slew other 6 deare 'in the Yle of Rowme'.

(Scottish History Society *Highland Papers* vol. IV, 1934)

After Clanranald finally relinquished Rum to the Macleans of Coll the island probably lost its status as a regional game reserve. However we find a strange superstition at work:

The mountains have some hundred of deer grazing in them. The natives gave me an account of a strange observation, which they say proves fatal to the posterity of Lachlin, a cadet of MacLean of Coll's family; that if any of them shoot at a deer on the mountain Finchra, he dies suddenly, or contracts some violent distemper, which soon puts a period to his life. They told me some instances to this purpose: whatever may be in it, there is none of the tribe above-named will ever offer to shoot the deer in that mountain.

(Martin *A Description of the Western Islands of Scotland, c.* 1695)

One can't help wondering if this was a convenient method of restricting Maclean access to their new resource. The number of deer was obviously in decline but there is contradiction between the evidence supplied by Walker in 1764 and that given by Thomas Pennant in 1772.

There is a large Herd of Red Deer kept upon the Island by the Proprietor.

(Walker *Report on the Hebrides*, 1764)

While Pennant quotes a local legend blaming the decline of deer numbers on predation by eagles.

> No wild quadrupeds are found, excepting stags: these animals once abounded here, but they are now reduced to eighty, by the eagles, who not only kill the fawns, but the old deer, seizing them between the horns, and terrifying them till they fall down some precipice, and become their prey.

> (Pennant *A Tour in Scotland and Voyage to the Hebrides*, 1772)

This story appears in Martin Martin in connection with North Uist *c*. 1695 and is endorsed by Edward Clarke in 1797. He is describing the crater of Orval:

> Near the bottom of this crater, Mr Maclean shewed me the remains of the snare used for taking the red deer, at a time when they were exceedingly numerous upon this island. About ten years ago, they became perfectly extinct in Rum. The natives themselves destroyed several of them; but the principal cause of their extirpation must be attributed to the eagles, who devoured not only the young, but the old ones themselves. One would think it incredible, that an eagle should venture to attack so large an animal as the stag of the great red deer. The mode in which the natives account for it is, that the eagles plunged upon the head of the intended prey, and fastened between his horns. This drove the stag to madness, and he would speedily rush headlong down a precipice; when the eagle disengaging himself during the fall, would return at leisure to mangle the carcase of the expiring victim.

> (Edward Daniel Clarke, 1797)

There is something unconvincing about this story. It has the air of an elaborate rationalisation and one cannot help feeling that the main cause of the destruction of deer was the expanding population of Rum in the eighteenth century. Deer were not only food, they were competitors for grazing. With a human population of between three and four hundred they would certainly be hunted during years of scarcity. The natives may have wished to conceal this from their chief and his agents, so the eagle became a convenient scapegoat. Population pressure must have quickly eradicated deer from the other Small Isles. The only reason they survived in Rum was because they were protected. In Eigg it was said:

> But of red deer there is not even a tradition.
>
> (Macpherson *Notes on Antiquities from the Island of Eigg*, 1878)

In the same vein Hugh Miller informs us of a Mr Greig:

> I visited the island of Eigg, in 1825 or 1826, for the purpose of shooting, and remained in it several days; and as there was a great scarcity of game, I amused myself in my wanderings by looking about for natural curiosities.

Deer could only survive against human competition if they were protected by powerful interests. In the *Old Statistical Account* M'Lean repeats the story about eagles and describes an elerig.

> In Rum there were formerly great numbers of deer; there was also a copse of wood, that afforded cover to their fawn from birds of prey, particularly from the eagle: While the wood throve, the deer also throve; now that the wood is totally destroyed, the deer are extirpated. Before the use of fire arms, their method of killing deer was as follows: On each side of a glen, formed by two mountains, stone dykes were begun pretty high in the mountains, and carried to the lower part of the valley, always drawing nearer, till within 3 or 4 feet of each other. From this narrow pass, a circular space was inclosed by a stone wall, of a height sufficient to confine the deer; to this place they were

109

pursued and destroyed. The vestige of one of these inclosures is still to be seen in Rum. . . .

Tradition says, that of old the islands forming this parish, had names sometimes given them different from those which they now bear . . . Rum was called Rioghachd na Forraiste Fiadhaich (the Kingdom of the Wild Forrest).

(M'Lean *Old Statistical Account,*
Parish of Small Isles, 1794)

Robertson was struck by this taboo-name given to Rum – Rioghachd na Forraiste Fiadhaich – the kingdom of the wild forest. He says:

Rioghachd seems a large word; perhaps Rum was a royal forest.

(Robertson 'Topography and
Traditions of Eigg', 1898)

It may once have been exactly that! If Dugald Macruari was king over the northern Hebrides in the 1250s perhaps he maintained Rum as his sporting preserve. Ostentatious display was an important political tool for mediaeval Hebridean chiefs; Dugald may have kept Rum as a deer forest in order to impress the island lords.

Surviving structures

What survives of all this in Rum? There certainly seems to be one, possibly two, of the stone enclosures into which the deer were driven (see Plate 8 and Map 10). However there are also long stretches of dyke with little stone cells. How are we to interpret these? Were the dykes built to regulate stock movements, or were they to channel deer in a hunt. Were the little stone cells actually shielings or hunting-seats? Unfortunately many of the structures are now very ruinous. However one such site is called Sron

Deer-traps in Rum

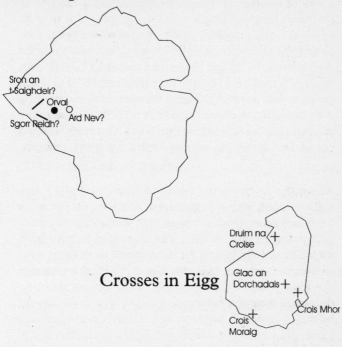

Sron an
t-Saighdeir?

Orval

Ard Nev?

Sgorr Reidh?

Crosses in Eigg

Druim na
Croise +

Glac an
Dorchadais +

+

Crois Mhor

Crois +
Moraig

Map 10

an t-Saighdeir. The word *saighdear* now means soldier, but it once meant archer. The place-name could indicate a former use. Archers may have occupied these seats or shooting-positions as the deer were driven in front of them. From the early seventeenth century guns started to replace bows.

Difficulties interpreting the structures are compounded by difficulties in interpreting later texts which tend to confuse the enclosures (into which the deer were driven) with the seats (from which hunters fired at the deer).

111

The mode in which these snares were constructed is this; a wall or rampart of stones was erected along the side of the mountain, flanking a considerable part of it near its basis; at either extremity of which a pit was formed, concealed by a circumference of the same stones which formed the rampart. In this pit the hunter stationed himself with his gun. A number of people were then employed to alarm the deer, who instantly taking to the mountain, and meeting with the wall, ran along the side of it till they came to the pit, in which the sentinels were posted, who easily selected one of them as they passed, and levelled him with his musket.

(Edward Daniel Clarke, 1797)

About the centre of the Island of Rum, long dikes may still be traced, which, beginning at considerable distances from each other, gradually approach, until at last they draw pretty near to one another. These are said to have been intended as toils [traps] for deer, which were once, as is well known, numerous in that island. To these enclosures the inhabitants collected them, and, forcing them by degrees to their narrowest recesses, they were finally caught by their pursuers. The places where these enclosures were made still maintain the names of Tigh'n Sealg, that is, the hunting-houses; so that it is likely that at the termination of the dikes, houses were erected, into which the deer were constrained to enter, and in this manner a number of them would be at once secured.

(Maclean *New Statistical Account,*
Parish of Small Isles, 1836)

It is ironic how, in the nineteenth century, once the people had been cleared, an élite turned Rum back into a hunting reserve. There was plenty of game, as long as there weren't many people.

There were almost always one or more carcases of deer slung between the trees. Against the kitchen wall, too, under shading boughs, abundance of feathered game, chiefly grouse, might always be seen hanging; and the supply of it was renewed from day to day. Against another wall different kinds of fish were hung.

(Waugh *The Limping Pilgrim*, 1882)

Falconry

Another type of hunting was falconry, which enjoyed equally high status. Hawks were expensive to acquire and their nesting-sites were valuable. Two of the four Small Isles were noted by Dean Monro in this respect.

SWYNES ILE. . . . a good falcon nest in it. . . .

KANNAY. . . . with a falcon nest in it.

(Monro *A Description of the Western Isles of Scotland* 1549)

Canna and Muck were church property and it is interesting that they were both expected to supply falcons as part of their render. Monro's view of Muck is endorsed by Martin Martin:

ISLE MUCK

. . . the hawks in the rocks here are reputed to be very good.

(Martin *A Description of the Western Islands of Scotland, c.* 1695)

In earlier times both Sea and Golden Eagles may have been taken from Rum:

Upon the Mountain Ascheval, we found a Nest of the Golden Eagle, the Falco chrysactos of Linnaeus, and brought away the young one.

(Walker *Report on the Hebrides*, 1764)

113

Massacre in Uamh Fhraing

When faced with the endless disorder and faction that disturbed the Isles after 1500 we are inclined to project the earlier Lordship as a period of political stability. As the documents of 1203 (Iona) and 1428 (Canna) imply this may not represent the true situation. However there is no doubt that the history of the Highlands and Islands in the sixteenth and seventeenth centuries makes grim reading. There does not seem to have been the same cultural flowering: the monasteries and churches were not maintained; the crosses and grave-slabs not commissioned. One example of the internecine clan warfare is the massacre of Uamh Fhraing in Eigg. This provides a sad comment on the unhappy political situation in the Isles after the collapse of the Lordship. I give the earliest accounts and descriptions from the nineteenth century, by which time the cave had become a tourist attraction.

> Thair is mony coves under the earth in this Ile, quhilk the cuntrie folkis uses as strenthis hiding thame and thair geir thairintill; quhairthrow it hapenit that in March, anno 1577, weiris and inmitie betwix the said Clan Renald and McCloyd Herreik, the people with ane callit Angus John McMudzartsonne, their capitane, fled to ane of the saidis coves, taking with thame thair wives, bairnis, and geir, quhairof McCloyd Herreik being advertisit landit with ane great armie in the said Ile, and came to the cove and pat fire thairto, and smorit the haill people thairin to the number of 395 persones, men, wyfe, and bairnis.
>
> (Skene *The Description of the Isles of Scotland*, 1577–95)

This account was written within a few years of the massacre and is confirmed by another in Macfarlane. Although often dated to the early seventeenth century these notes were probably made by Timothy Pont, the cartographer, during his voyages to the islands in the 1590s:

> They perished and destroyed with the smoak of the fyre the number of both of men and woemen an barnes within ane Cove or den that is in this Illand of the Inhabitants by McLeod of Harie being in warrs against him for that tyme, and taking this place for their safetie and refuge.
>
> (Mitchell (ed.) *Macfarlane's Geographical Collections*, vol II, p. 176, ?1590s)

Like many another gruesome site the massacre cave eventually became a tourist attraction.

> The sight of the walls, still blackened by the smoke, and, above all, the quantity of human bones and skulls scattered on the ground, were for us too striking proofs of the truth of that horrid catastrophe; and the effect produced on us by the unexpected discovery of these human skulls, and the horror which momentarily overcame us, can be easier imagined than described.
>
> (Necker de Saussure *A Voyage to the Hebrides*, 1807)

> The floor, for about a hundred feet inwards from the narrow vestibule, resembles that of a charnel-house. At almost every step we come upon heaps of human bones grouped together . . . They are of a brownish, earthy hue, here and there tinged with green; the skulls, with the exception of a few broken fragments, have disappeared; for travellers in the Hebrides have of late years been numerous and curious; and many a museum . . . exhibits, in a grinning skull, its memorial of the Massacre at Eigg. We find, too, further marks of visitors in the single bones separated from the heaps and scattered over the area; but enough still remains to show, in the general disposition of the remains, that the hapless islanders died under the walls in families, each little group separated by a few feet from

115

the others. . . . And beneath every heap we find, at the depth . . . of a few inches, the remains of the straw-bed upon which the family had lain, largely mixed with the smaller bones of the human frame, ribs and vertebrae, and hand and feet bones; occasionally, too, with fragments of unglazed pottery, and various other implements of a rude housewifery.

(Miller *The Cruise of the Betsey*, 1845)

Miller, though, had a sense of humour, and, like many early travellers to the Hebrides, he had experienced the discomforts of a Highland cottage.

I am inclined to believe, from the appearance of the place, that smoke could scarcely have been the real agent of destruction: then, as now, it would have taken a great deal of pure smoke to smother a Highlander.

Ever the practical man, he went on to offer a more scientific explanation.

It may be perhaps deemed more probable, that the huge fire of rafter and roof-tree piled close against the opening, and rising high over it, would draw out the oxygen within as its proper food, till at length all would be exhausted; and life would go out for want of it, like the flame of a candle under an upturned jar.

Some later writers have voiced scepticism about the date of the massacre and the number of people killed. Alasdair Crotach is traditionally cast as the Macleod villain but he was dead long before 1577 and the massacre is not recorded by the Macdonald historians. In 1794 Donald M'Lean wrote of the cave:

About 40 skulls have been lately numbered here. It is probable a greater number was destroyed; if so, their neighbouring friends may have carried them off for burial in consecrated ground.

Despite M'Lean's assertion it is possible that the number of people massacred was actually no more than forty. In 1794 the tourist invasion of the Highlands was only just beginning; perhaps visitors were not helping themselves to gruesome relics as freely as they were fifty years later. There are further reasons for doubting the massacre figure of 395.

Skene's same anonymous author says that Eigg could raise sixty men to the wars – without saying how it had achieved such a miraculous recovery in such a short space of time! A levy of sixty men suggests a total population for Eigg of about 300. This population would have been spread through the island, perhaps half of it on the better lands around Cleadale and Laig. Traditional accounts of the massacre usually give as its prelude the maltreatment of some Eigg women on Eilean Chathastail off the south end of the island. It seems most probable that those who avenged this, and then repaired to the cave during the Macleod reprisal, were local families from Grulin, Galmisdale and Sanda. It is difficult to see why families from Cleadale and Howlin would trek south to Uamh Fhraing when they had other caves closer to hand. In this case the massacre figure might well approximate to the number of skulls seen in 1794, but even at forty the slaughter is still gruesome. The bones were eventually removed but another child's skull was found in a corner some years ago.

As if this disaster was not enough, in October 1588 Lachlan MacLean of Duart

accompanied with a great number of thieves, broken men, and sorners of Clans, besides the number of one hundred Spaniards came, bodin in feir of war, to his Majesty's proper isles of Canna, Rum, Eigg and the Isle of Elennole, and, after they had sorned wrecked and spoiled the said whole Isles, they treasonably raised fire and in most barbarous shameful and cruel manner, burnt the same Isles with the whole men women and children being thereinto, not sparing the pupils and infants . . . The like barbarous and shameful cruelty has seldom been heard of among Christians in any kingdom or age, the said Lachlan being moved hereunto in respect the inhabitants of the said Isles were his Majesty's proper tenants destitute of the comfort and assistance of the clannit men of the Isles to participate with them in their own defence.

> (Robertson 'Topography and Traditions of Eigg',
> 1898, quoting the Register of the Privy Council,
> 3 January 1589, with modernised spellings)

The implication is that because Canna, Rum, Eigg and Elennole (Muck?) were technically held by the Crown, they could not rely on support from their fellow clansmen elsewhere in the Hebrides, and so lay defenceless before Lachlan Maclean. The event is elaborated in the legal proceedings of January 1590–1 which describe the bitter feud between Angus Macdonald of Dunyveg and Lachlan Maclean of Duart. It was claimed that Maclean had, with the help of Spanish troops from the Armada,

burned with fire the lands of Canna, Rum, Eigg and Muck, and harried the same; he slew and cruelly murdered Hector McCane Channaniche and Donald Bayne his brother, with a great number of wives, bairns and poor labourers of the ground, about eight or nine score of souls, who had escaped the fire, was not spared by his bloody sword.

> (R. Pitcairn, *Ancient Criminal Trials in
> Scotland*, 1883) [spellings modernised]

It would be wrong to imagine the Small Isles in the Middle Ages as any form of island paradise. If an enemy could come by sea your island became a trap, not a refuge. The people of the Small Isles would be reminded of this unpleasant geopolitical fact after the 1745 Rising.

Ownership

The Macdonald Lordship of the Isles was finally forfeited in 1493. In the following century the political and ecclesiastical structure of the Hebrides fell apart. Before 1493 there had been a political order in the west, prone to internal feuding certainly, but with a clear apex and a carefully defined hierarchy. Families had jostled for power, but there was a system, maintained by the dynasty of the Lords of the Isles, within which each family had their place. After 1493 this was never resuscitated. The situation reverted to one of warring factions and unbridled ambition. The Scottish realm callously exploited clan divisions while rival dynasties such as the Campbells and the Mackenzies moved into the political vacuum.

Before the Reformation there had also been an ecclesiastical structure which was intimately tied to the Lordship. After the forfeiture and the Reformation the great estates of the church fell prey to lay interests. Lands that had formerly belonged to Iona or the Bishop of the Isles now came into the clutches of the local laird. Canna and Muck were lost to the church. We can follow some of these changes through the early topographical accounts. Authors distinguish between those to whom the land 'pertains', and those who had it in their 'handis', that is between legal ownership and physical possession.

Rum

RONIN. Sixteen myle northwast from the ile of Coll, lyes ane ile, callit Ronin ile . . . This iyle . . . pertains to M'Kenabrey of Colla.

(Monro *A Description of the Western Isles of Scotland*, 1549)

119

Romb . . . perteinis heretablie to ane Barron callit the Laird
of Challow [Coll], quha is of McClanes kin, but is possest
and in the handis of Clan-Rannald.

(Skene *The Description of the Isles of Scotland*, 1577–95)

Rhum . . . This Illand appertaines to the Laird of Colla.

(Mitchell (ed.) *Macfarlane's Geographical
Collections*, p. 176, ?1590s)

Rum may have been acquired by the Macleans of Coll in the
mid-fifteenth century but it was in Clanranald's hands at the
end of the sixteenth century and probably still
maintained as a hunting reserve. As late as 1626 the Bishop
of the Isles stated that Rum only had two 'tounes' although
in 1625 the Franciscan missionary Cornelius Ward reckoned
it had three. Since Ward actually visited the island his evidence
is more valuable although the fact that he only converted
seventeen people suggests the population was still low. Once
the Macleans of Coll were firmly established the role of Rum
as a deer forest seems to have declined and the Macleans
may have deliberately planted the island with loyal tenants
from Coll and elsewhere. By 1801 some nine hamlets appear
on Langlands' map and in Pennant's description. The
population figures show a corresponding increase.

Canna

KANNAY . . . pertines to the Abbot of Colmkill.

(Monro *A Description of the Western
Isles of Scotland*, 1549)

The Abbatis landis within the Clanrannaldis boundis.
Item, the Ile of Cannay.

(Rental of the Bishopric of the Isles,
1561, in *Collectanea de Rebus Albanicis*)

Canna . . . It perteins to the Bischop of the Iles, but the said Clan-Rannald hes it in possessioun . . .

> (Skene *The Description of the Isles of Scotland,* 1577–95)

Cainna ane Illand pertaining to the Captaine of the Clanronnald.

> (Mitchell (ed.) *Macfarlane's Geographical Collections,* p. 177, ?1590s)

Cana ane small Iland belonging to the Abbott of Icolmikill and now in the possessione of Johne Mccloyd.

> (Report by the Bishop of the Isles, 1626, in *Collectanea de Rebus Albanicis*)

Argyll gained the feudal superiority of Canna in 1627 and from 1672 it was leased by Clanranald. The charter by which he held it is extremely interesting because it contains a clause which looks like a throwback to earlier mediaeval charters of the island. The contract between the Earl of Argyll and Clanranald in 1672 stipulated:

> and for serving the Earl, when required, with a galley of sixteen oars, sufficiently appointed with men and necessaries for thirty days yearly between the isle of Canna and Icolmkill.

> (*Fourth Report of the Royal Commission on Historical Manuscripts,* 1874)

It is not obvious why Argyll would want the galley to ply between Canna and Iona (Icolmkill), another peripheral isle in his large dominions. It is more likely that what we have here is a clause lifted from older charters when the island belonged to Iona. We might expect that former tenants were obliged to provide a galley to ferry Canna's surplus produce to Iona.

Muck and Eilean nan Each

SWYNES ILE . . . It perteynis to the Bishope of the iles.

> (Monro *A Description of the Western Isles of Scotland*, 1549)

THE HORSE IYLE . . . perteining to the Bishope of the iles.

> (ibid.)

Rentale of Bischopis landis within the Illis.
. . . Item, the Ille callit Ellanamwk, possest be M'Aen of Ardnamurchane.

> (Rental of the Bishopric of the Isles, 1561, in *Collectanea de Rebus Albanicis*)

Ellan na Muk . . . perteins also to the foirsaid Bischop, and is possesst be the Laird of Ardinmwrthe callit Maken. It . . . payis to the said Laird and his factors aucht score bollis victuall, quhairof four score to the Bischop and four score to the Laird.

> (Skene *The Description of the Isles of Scotland*, 1577–95)

Illand Muck . . . appertaines to the Bishop of the Illes of the highlands of Scotland

> (Mitchell (ed.) *Macfarlane's Geographical Collections*, p. 175, ?1590s)

Muck ane small Iland conteining onlie tua tounes, belonges to the Laird of Coll, peyis ane chalder of beir.

> (Report by the Bishop of the Isles, 1626, in *Collectanea de Rebus Albanicis*)

After the Reformation, Muck seems to have been possessed, if not owned, by the Macians of Ardnamurchan, and even, briefly, by Glengarry. It passed, eventually, to the Lairds of Coll although the Ardnamurchan connection resonated through later years.

Eigg

Eg . . . perteins to the Clan Rannald.

(Skene *The Description of the Isles of Scotland*, 1577–95)

Eigg was the only one of the Small Isles to remain in the possession of the same family from the early mediaeval period to the beginning of the nineteenth century. It descended from the Macruaris to Clanranald, although, as we have seen in Chapter 3, about a third of the island passed to the Macdonalds of Morar from 1498. This family was an offshoot of Clanranald and always closely associated with the main branch.

5

The Small Isles and the '45

THE ISLANDS OF EIGG and Canna were Clanranald property and therefore became involved in the 1745 Rising through the participation of the leading clansmen. Allan Macdonald of Morar was lieutenant-colonel or second-in-command of Clanranald's regiment. His family had a long association with Eigg and owned part of the island. A branch of the Macdonalds of Morar were the Macdonalds of Laig. We do not know much about their participation in the actual campaign, although a brother of Laig is said to have been killed, but we learn more about them after the Rising, particularly in Bishop Forbes's compilation *The Lyon in Mourning*. Robert Forbes was an ardent Jacobite who made it his life's work to collect materials about the Rising from participants and eye-witnesses.

On 10 July 1749 Forbes wrote to Alexander Macdonald, the poet.

> You told me you intended to take up your abode in Egg or Canna, which if you do, then it will be in your power to

make up an exact account of the severe pillaging and plunderings that were committed in these islands. You know I like much to have everything minutely and circumstantially narrated. Forget not then to give the names of those who were principally concerned in pillaging Egg and Canna, such as officers of sogers [soldiers], commanders of ships, sloops, or yachts. Be mindful likewise to make as exact a calculation as you can of the damages sustained by the inhabitants of these two islands. In a word, send me an account of everything you can have well vouched. I need not point out particulars to you; for well do you know what I want and what will suit my taste.

(Paton (ed.) *Lyon in Mourning*
vol. II, pp. 336–7)

In considering Alexander's reply we have to take into account the fact that the poet was not just another ardent Jacobite. He was virulently anti-Hanoverian and his judgement became more coloured than most. That said, the evidence is contemporary and he was bailie of Canna, which gave him good opportunity to find out from local people what really happened.

On 22 April 1751, Alexander Macdonald visited Robert Forbes and gave him a handwritten account of events in Canna and Eigg. The first part concerns Canna, where John Macdonald of Laig held the lands of Tarbert from Clanranald.

Upon the 3d of April 1746, Lieutennant Thomas Brown, an Irish gentleman . . . did sail with a tender from the *Baltimore* man of war by Captain Fergusons order . . . came to the haven of Canna, and after sending for James M'Donald, bailie of the Island, and uncle to Glenaladal, told him he was sent by Captains Ferguson and Dove for some fresh beef and mutton, vizt., 20 fat cows and so many wedders. . . . He had 60 armed men at his heels; the flower of the Islanders was with the Prince; soe that the bailie judged it safer both for himself and inhabitants to grant his request, and consequently sent off to the meadows for the above number of cattle, and took them up in proportion to the number of tenements the Isle consisted of. But being wind-bound for 4 days in Canna harbour, behold! they complained to the said bailie the beef of the cattle slaughter'd stunk, and that the country should give them the same number over again. The bailie reckoned this both unjust and cruel, and that it was enough for the poor inhabitants to gratify him of what they received already. Upon which the officer was petted and said with a rage he knew where and by whom he woud be served. He meant Laaig's cattle, whom he heard was in the Prince's army. So he hurls away his 60 armed men, gathers all the cattle of the Isle into a particular creek, shot 60 of the best dead, threw the old beef overboard and woud not allow the poor distressed owners to finger a gobbet of it, no, not a single tripe of the first or former. 40 of the last cattle belonged to Laaig, 20 to the tennants.

There then follows an account of how the crew of the '*Commodore*' tried to rape the women of the island, all of whom seem to have escaped by hiding, although the ordeal caused one wife to miscarry and die.

After the battle of Culloden:

General Campbell . . . calls at Canna, and hurls away the honest bailie prisoner into his ship without allowing him to speak for himself, or as much time as to shift himself or take leave of his wife. [Afterwards] he was brought . . . back to Canna. Then he believed he would be liberate, but instead thereof they caus'd 40 of his cows to be slaughtered, would not permit him as much liberty as goe ashore to take leave of his wife or children, or to bring his cloaths with him, but brought him prisoner to London where he continued upwards of 12 month.

Alexander also gives an account of events in Eigg where the navy boats were pursuing refugee Jacobites:

Sometime about the 20th of June 1746, Captain Duff went, be orders of his superiour officer, to the Island of Eigg . . . for executing the disarming act; called the inhabitants into one place, and were strictly charged to carry with them all their arms upon their peril. They conveend, delivered up some arms, but got onely recepts for them. The poor people afterwards looked on themselves out of the reach of any danger. But then some weeks thereafter, Captains Ferguson and Duff went to Eigg to look after one Captain John MacDonald, commonly called Doctor, brother to the late Kinlochmoydoirt, whom they heard to be under covert in the Isle. After examining some of the inhabitants to that purpose, they stifly denied the Captain to be there with their knowledge. With this they sends about 100 men, divided into small corps, in search of him. One Mr Daniel MacQueen, minister of the Gospell at the Isle of Rum, happend to be then at Eigg, being a parte of his parish, and was both agent and interpreter 'twixt the inhabitants and the enemie. He, Mr MacQueen, well knew the very place where MacDonald was hiding himself, and understood by reason of the narrow scrutiny they were resolved to make after him, they would fish him out. Therefore he goes himself in person where he was, and, after explaining him the danger he was under, prevailed with him to surrender and yield himself prisoner to Captain Fergusone. Accordingly he did. He was first well us'd. But behold the unluckiness of the poor Eigg people; for one of the party that was traversing the country back and forward, glens and mountains, found out so many stands of arms that they reserved for their own use. Captain Ferguson did not seem to be much disobliged at this; but reflected that, notwithstanding what they formerly delivered him, they still reserved their full compliment. However, he bespeaks Captain MacDonald, the doctor, and earnestly desires him,

127

for the poor people's own safety and good of the country, he shoud call them all and perswad them to come in, the whole inhabitants with their whole arms of all kinds, and that he would give them full protections for both their persons and effects that woud save them against any future danger: otherwise, and if they shoud not come in heartily, all of them come to the years of discretion and to the age of bearing arms, he woud immediately . . . cause his men burn all their houses, destroy all their cattle and carry the whole men away. Mr MacQueen advises Captain MacDonald to send for the men with the remainder of their arms in the terms spoken by Ferguson. He sends some dozen of lads for them. They were seen comeing in a body. Immediatly Ferguson ordered Captain MacDonald to be seizd upon and made prisoner of, brought into a house to be confin'd thereto for ane hour. The men laid down their arms, such of them as had any. The few old people that came among them were picked out and dismist home. Then Captain MacDonald was brought out of the house, was stript of all his cloaths to the skin, even of his shoes and stockins, brought aboard the *Furnace*, barisdall'd in a dark dungeon. And to the poor people's additional misfortune, there was a devilish paper found about him, containing a list of all the Eigg folk that were in the Princes service. Then that catalogue was read by their patronimicks in the name of giving the promised protection, which ilk one answered cheerfully, and was drawn out into another rank, so that there were noe fewer than 38 snatched aboard the man of war, were brought to London, from thence transported to Jamaica, where the few that lives of them continue slaves as yet. Many of them dyed and starved ere they arrove at the Thames. The most of them were marryed men, leaving throng families behind them. They slaughtered all their cattle, pillaged all their houses ore [ere?] they left the isle, and ravished a girl or two. This relation I had from the bailie of Canna and the bailie of Eigg.

(Paton (ed.) *Lyon in Mourning* vol. III, 1895)

The word 'barisdall'd' derives from an invention of Coll Macdonald of Barrisdale who used an unpleasant type of iron stocks to secure any who fell foul of him. It is ironic to find this word used in a Hanoverian context although by now many Jacobites were convinced that the Barrisdales were turncoats.

In response to Robert Forbes's open-ended invitation Alexander Macdonald took the opportunity of showing just how unpleasant Hanoverian vengeance could be. While Forbes was something of a stickler for exactitude this is not a trait one would normally associate with Alexander: his passion burned fiercely and his poetry suggests a predisposition to bend the truth to the cause.

Captain Ferguson's log for the *Furnace* presents rather a different picture. For Saturday 31 May 1746 he records:

> at 3 pm Sent the Boats maned ashore on Egg Island for Arms.

The next day, Sunday 1 June, with the wind variable westerly

> the Boats Returned with 50 Stand of Arms and 16 prisoners.

As Alexander's detailed descriptions may exaggerate, so Ferguson's laconic entries probably understate, the nature of reprisal. For these reasons it is helpful to be able to point to some independent evidence for Hanoverian conduct in the Small Isles.

Firstly we have David Bruce's rentals and lists of tenant arrears made in 1748. It is significant that Canna had the highest ratio of arrears, proportionally nearly four times as great as those in Arisaig. This suggests that of all the Clanranald Estates, Canna may have suffered the most.

Secondly there are government records which help us determine the fate of those men taken from Eigg and imprisoned. In a fascinating article 'Eigg and the '45', published in the *Clan Donald Magazine* (no. 13), David McDonald has described what happened to the men from Eigg whom he was able to identify in official records. By further analysis of the data he gives we can gain a brief insight into the lives of some of these poor islanders.

Such men were not likely to have had any choice about participating in the campaign. Recruitment in the Highlands during the eighteenth century was not a voluntary matter. Military levy had probably always been an obligation owed by tenant to landlord, however it is only in recent times that we find much record of it. Some landlords ruthlessly exploited their tenants for military service.

The Eigg men probably served in the contingent brought by Allan Macdonald of Morar at the very start of the campaign. They came from all over the island. Most were local although they included men born in Kinlochmoidart, Morvern, Morar, South Uist and Inverness. Most are described as farmers or involved in agriculture. The average age was thirty-eight and the average height five feet six inches. These figures are intriguing. Given that, at the time, half the population of the island was under twenty, the men are older than one might expect, and not strikingly tall. Highlanders had served as mercenaries in Ireland for hundreds of years, particularly in the latter half of the sixteenth century. There are plenty of references to the desire of their Irish paymasters for tall men, presumably on the grounds that they were likely to be stronger and more formidable. The Eigg contingent were surprisingly old, chosen either because of their experience or because they could better be spared. We even know the complexions of sixteen of them: ten fair, six brown.

Some probably died in the dreadful conditions on board the prison hulks in the Thames. In a medical inspection of August 1747 a number of men in the hold were not even strong enough to climb on deck. Of the rest some were transported to Jamaica and Barbados and some were released.

The question arises as to how Captain John Macdonald happened to have on him a list of all those who had taken part in the Rising. At first sight it seems an example of almost unbelievable stupidity. John was in hiding, had been persuaded to give himself up, yet kept about him a list of those others involved in the campaign. Now it is perfectly possible that such a list actually existed. We have a comparable list for Clanranald's mainland estate which was apparently drawn up in 1745 and first printed in 1819. However what would possess John to carry this list into captivity with him?

There is however an alternative explanation which is that the story is an attempt to cover up some contemporary double-dealing. The list may simply be an invention to hide complicity in the Hanoverian expedition. This is not a matter of taking the moral high ground. We have plenty of examples of cover-up in our own age and there is no reason to assume the eighteenth century was any different. Human nature will always be challenged by selfish impulse. It is perhaps a pity that historians of the Jacobite period have cast it in such black and white terms. Of course there was the noblest loyalty, but there was also the foulest treachery, as was recognised by Jacobites at the time. Why should there not have been every shade of compromise and accommodation in between?

At the time Highland society was riven by faction and intrigue. Culloden was a political and cultural disaster, as well as a military defeat. All those who had participated faced enormous problems of personal safety, the physical and economic wellbeing of their families and the destruction of their property and possessions. It is no wonder that reactions varied widely. We see the whole range of human nature, from the blind and simple loyalty of men like Borrodale and Glenaladale, through the post-Culloden coolness of Morar and Clanranald, to the suspected treachery of Coll of Barrisdale. The atmosphere became one of *sauve qui peut*, every man for himself, and of course not everyone behaved in an equally honourable manner.

Captain John's brother, Donald of Kinlochmoidart, was executed at Carlisle in October 1746. David Macdonald writes that two of the Eigg men probably turned King's Evidence, were put into the custody of a Mr Dick and released on 11 June 1747. It may be significant that Captain John was also placed in the custody of Mr Dick and released on the same day.

Now there is absolutely no proof as to who, if anyone, was guilty of treachery but equally there is no doubt that some came out of the Rising better than others. Laig himself remained at liberty and appears in Arisaig in 1748–49 when he helped value Clanranald's woods. Captain John Macdonald returned to live in Kinlochmoidart.

John MacDougall, Angus MacMartin and others were among those transported to the West Indies. Unlike Glenaladale or Alexander Macdonald or Kinlochmoidart they do not participate in the Jacobite myth. There is no room for them in Bishop Forbes' pantheon. They survived, but they had lost everything – their children, their wives, their homes – for the sake of the politics of their chiefs.

Jacobite historians have focused on simple and unswerving loyalty. This is not an attempt to denigrate such loyalty but simply to point out a more complex truth. It was the Jacobites themselves who first imprisoned Barrisdale, long before the government ever did. Part of this more complex truth is that this was not a democratic war; some suffered terribly, and, as in all wars, a few may have sacrificed others in order to save themselves.

The visits of the Royal Navy boats to the Small Isles must have had a cathartic effect. Most Hebrideans had been immune from external attack for about 800 years. Since the Vikings, the only people they had to fear were each other. Now their enemy came by sea. The islands, instead of being a refuge, became a trap. For the islanders this must have been one of the most critical psychological effects of defeat. It must have helped them realise the military impossibility of a Jacobite restoration.

6

The Economic Base 1500–1850

F ROM THE SIXTEENTH AND seventeenth centuries we have a number of topographical accounts. Dean Monro, Timothy Pont (Macfarlane's Geographical Collections), and Skene's anonymous author were all concerned with describing each island's principal characteristics. They gave length and breadth, valuation, produce, number of fighting men and economic resources. From about 1695, when Martin Martin wrote, our sources become far more revealing. We are no longer confined to economic reports and factual descriptions; now we have accounts by the first tourists in the area, people who came here for pleasure rather than necessity. We no longer deal with bare facts, we meet judgements.

Traditional society in the Small Isles was agricultural. It is only at the very end of their history that we meet with semi-industrial activities such as kelp-burning. When the agricultural base could no longer support the population the islands' economy started to fall apart. This process began in the second half of the eighteenth century. With the start of the nineteenth century came large-scale clearance in Muck and Rum, and terminal decline everywhere. Many of the circumstances are individual to each island and whatever fortune it enjoyed under successive owners. Much of this has already been described by other authors, and I am not going to repeat this. Instead I am going to try and paint a picture of the traditional society of the Small Isles just before its demise.

In the sections that follow I have arranged extracts by theme, by island and generally in chronological order. I have dealt only with fundamental issues: land-holding, agriculture, industry, trees, fuel and housing.

Land-holding

David Bruce was a government agent and surveyor who travelled extensively throughout the Highlands and Islands after the 1745 Rising. He conducted a series of judicial rentals which give us our first real evidence of land-holding conditions.

> John McAlpin, Donald McLeland, Niven McAlpin and John McInnes all Tenants in Sandymore in the Island of Egg Who being all Sworn & Examined Depose That they possess equally without a written Tack the five penny Land of Sandymore pertaining to the Estate of Clanronald For which they are lyable to pay equally amongst them one hundred Merks Scotts yearly of money Rent, Each of them one Sheep, or Two Merks Scotts for the same . . . All which they Declare to be truth as they shall Answer to God And that they Cannot write.

> (Kirktoun, Eigg, 20 August 1748, David Bruce's Rental (E 744/1/1))

David Bruce also took depositions from twenty-four

tenants in Canna. Two of these had very substantial holdings, the rest held small parcels of land in Kirktoun ranging from a half-pennyland to one-and-a-quarter pennylands. Of these small tenants only one, Neil McNeil, the schoolmaster, could write. Donald McAlpin, the blacksmith, held a half-pennyland of Kirktoun 'In Virtue of a Verball Agreement' with the factor. Almost everyone was two or three years in arrears with their rent. Between the chief and most of his tenants there was an enormous economic and social gulf: the former also held all the levers of cultural and legal power.

The eighteenth century finally saw the decline of the pennyland as the unit of rural reckoning. We begin to meet references to acres, and rentals in terms of pence per acre. 'Improvement' was on the horizon.

Rum . . . is let for little more than a penny per acre . . .
Eig . . . is let for about 3d. p. Acre . . .
Canna . . . is let at about 4d.$^1/_2$ p. Acre.

(Walker *Report on the Hebrides*, 1764)

The rent of Rum is not great. Mr Maclean declared, that he should be very rich, if he could set his land at two-pence halfpenny an acre.

(Johnson *A Journey to the Western Islands of Scotland*, 1773)

Agriculture

Canna

KANNAY . . . ane ile callit Kannay, faire maine land, foure myle lange, inhabit and manurit . . . guid for corne, fishing and grassing.

(Monro *A Description of the Western Isles of Scotland*, 1549)

136

This Cainna is verie profitable and fertill both of corne and milk.

> (Mitchell (ed.) *Macfarlane's Geographical Collections*, p. 177, ?1590s)

This Ile is gude baith for corn and all kind of bestiall.

> (Skene *The Description of the Isles of Scotland*, 1577–95)

The whole fruitful in corn and grass.

> (Martin *A Description of the Western Islands of Scotland*, c. 1695)

Canna . . . This Island . . . is one of the most beautifull Islands in all the the Highlands fit both for Corn and pasture, and is capable of great Improvement being Centrical to most of the Western Islands.

> (Bruce, Report in *Hardwicke Papers*, c. 1750)

The Island contains 10 Ploughs and there is a great deal of Ground also dug with the Spade. It exports a good many Cattle, but no other Article.

> (Walker *Report on the Hebrides*, 1764)

Ploughs . . . in Canna and Sand Island, 7.

> (M'Lean *Old Statistical Account*, 1794)

As soon as we had time to cast our eyes about, each shore appeared pleasing to humanity; verdant, and covered with hundreds of cattle: both sides gave a full idea of plenty, for the verdure was mixed with very little rock, and scarcely any heath: but a short conversation with the natives soon dispelled this agreeable error: they were at this very time in such want, that numbers for a long time had neither bread nor meal for their poor babes . . .

The crops had failed here the last year: but the little corn sown at present had a promising aspect: and the potatoes are the best I had seen: but these were not fit for use. The isles I fear annually experience a temporary famine: perhaps from improvidence, perhaps from eagerness to increase their stock of cattle, which they can easily dispose of to satisfy the demands of a landlord, or the oppressions of an agent. The people of Cannay export none, but sell them to the numerous busses, who put into this *portus salutis* [safe haven] on different occasions.

The cattle are of a middle size, black, long-legged, and have thin staring manes from the neck along the back, and up part of the tail. They look well, for in several parts of the islands they have good warm recesses to retreat to in winter. About sixty head are exported annually.

Each couple of milk cows yielded at an average of seven stones of butter and cheese: two thirds of the first and one of the last. The cheese sold at three and six pence a stone; the butter at eight shillings.

Here are very few sheep: but horses in abundance. . . . Here are plenty of poultry and of eggs.

It is said that the factor has in a manner banished sheep, because there is no good market for them; so that he does his best to deprive the inhabitants of cloathing as well as food. At present they supply themselves with wool from Rum, at the rate of eight pence the pound.

(Pennant A Tour in Scotland and
Voyage to the Hebrides, 1772)

This island, together with Sandy Island adjoining, are both very fertile, yielding great crops of potatoes, and barley or bear. From 100 to 200 quarters of barley or bear are annually disposed of, and about 3,200 bushels of potatoes, – being all the produce of the island, over and above the quantity which the inhabitants require for their own maintenance. The island is all clothed with verdure. The grass is fine and short, and well adapted for the rearing of black-cattle, of which a good many are annually sent to the markets in the south and sold.

(Maclean New Statistical Account, 1836)

The Revd Donald Maclean, who wrote the entry for the Small Isles in the *New Statistical Account*, took an overly optimistic view. In Canna the lands of Keill were cleared in 1849 and the families moved to Sanday. By 1861 many of them had gone completely and the population of Canna almost halved.

Rum

Rhum is ane big Illand . . . containing therintill but two tounes of Cornelands. One of these two tounes upon the Northwestsyde of this bigg Illand of Rhum And another toune on the West and southwestsyde theroff. The toune which is on the Northwest syde theroff is called Kilmoir in Rhum and the other Glenhairie in Rhum, the Illand is verie profitable for there is abundance of butter, cheese and milk in this Illand for there is no cornelands in it, but such as doth grow in these two tounes forsaid, but it is verie good for goods to feed intill in respect that it is full of muires, mossis, glenns hills and verie bigg mountaines

> (Mitchell (ed.) *Macfarlane's Geographical Collections*, p. 176, ?1590s)

Romb is ane Ile of small profit.

> (Skene *The Description of the Isles of Scotland*, 1577–95)

This isle . . . is mountainous and heathy, but the coast is arable and fruitful.

> (Martin *A Description of the Western Islands of Scotland*, c. 1695)

It contains at least, 15,360 English Statute Acres, of which there is a very small Proportion that has ever been cultivated; not above 1,500 Acres; for there is not a Plough in the Island; the Inhabitants cultivating their little Fields on the Sea Shore, entirely with the Spade. It may contain 3,000 Acres of coarse moorish and mossy Grounds capable of being [brought] into Culture, but the Remainder, by far the greatest part, may be judged wholly irreclaimable, consisting of Steep Mountains, deep Mosses and Tracks [Tracts?] of Land overspread with Rocks. (The whole Island is rented at present for about £80 so that it is let for little more than a penny per acre.)

(Walker *Report on the Hebrides*, 1764)

Ploughs . . . in Rum, 2; but they labour all with the spade, except two small fields.

(M'Lean *Old Statistical Account*, 1794)

In a Highland context the word spade tends to mean *cas-chrom* which is an angled wooden foot-plough.

Although he did not visit it Dr Samuel Johnson learned of Rum from young Maclean of Coll, son of the proprietor, whose company he enjoyed for several days.

Its owner represents it as mountainous, rugged, and barren. In the hills there are red deer.

(Johnson *A Journey to the Western Islands of Scotland*, 1773)

Early observers all agreed that the climate and soil of Rum were harsh and unsuitable for agriculture.

It is an Island of an unfavourable Climate, being much colder, by Reason of the Height of its Mountains, and much more subject to Rains and Winds, than the neighbouring Islands of Egg and Canna, which are lower Land. These Disadvantages of Climate, with its deep wet Soil, must prevent it from being ever profitable in the Production of Corn or Cattle.

(Walker *Report on the Hebrides*, 1764)

> Rum is a considerable island, or rather one continued rock . . . It . . . grazes cattle and sheep.
>
> (Knox *A Tour through the Highlands of Scotland and the Hebride Isles in 1786*)

In such a marginal economic landscape the islanders had to turn to whatever opportunity offered.

> There is a great Number of Goats kept upon the Island, and here I found an Article of Oeconomy generally unknown in other Places. The People of Rum carefully collect the Hair of their Goats, and after sorting it, send it to Glasgow where it is sold from 1sh. to 2sh. and 6d. p. pound according to its Fineness, and there it is manufactured into Wigs, which are sent to America.
>
> (Walker *Report on the Hebrides*, 1764)

The people of Rum also seem to have specialised in horse-breeding:

> The horses are very small, but of a breed eminent for beauty. Col, not long ago, bought one of them from a tenant; who told him, that as he was of a shape uncommonly elegant, he could not sell him but at a high price; and that whoever had him should pay a guinea and a half.
>
> (Johnson *A Journey to the Western Islands of Scotland*, 1773)

> Horses are reared for sale in Rum only: They are hardy and high mettled, though of a small size.
>
> (M'Lean *Old Statistical Account, Parish of Small Isles*, 1794)

Settlement sites were largely decided by geography. They were coastal, where the land might be more level, or the sea have a beach.

The surface of Rum is in a manner covered with heath,

and in a state of nature: the heights rocky. There is very little arable land, excepting about the nine little hamlets that the natives have grouped in different places; near which the corn is sown in diminutive patches, for the tenants here run-rig as in Cannay.

(Pennant *A Tour in Scotland and Voyage to the Hebrides*, 1772)

In a map of Argyllshire by George Langlands in 1801 there are nine settlements named on Rum. They are Samhnan Insir, Camas Pliasgaig, Kilmory, Guirdil, Harris, Papadil, Dibidil, Cove (that is, Laimhrig by Bagh na h-Uamha) and Kinlochscresort. Raonapoll is marked with a settlement symbol but no name is given. Edward Clarke describes Guirdil in 1797:

We took the long boat . . . and approached Rum. The approach is bold, with high precipitate cliffs, almost perpendicular, and yet covered with a green verdure, on whose fearful crags sheep were seen feeding. . . . A few huts, with a small boat or two, drawn up upon the beach, constitute what the natives term one of their villages.

(Edward Daniel Clarke, 1797)

Writing of Kinloch, Edwin Waugh says that there is:

A meadow of about four acres, at the head of the bay. This is the greatest piece of level and cultivated land which I have seen upon all the island up to this time; except at Kilmory, the site of the ancient church and village of that name, where there is another piece of level grass land, about the same extent. With these exceptions, and three or four smaller tracts of level farm land at Harris, at Gouridale, and at Papadale, almost all the island consists of wild, heathery, mountainous land.

(Waugh *The Limping Pilgrim*, 1882)

142

The little corn and potatoes they raise is very good; but so small is the quantity of bere and oats that there is not a fourth part produced to supply their annual wants: all the subsistence the poor people have besides, is curds, milk and fish. They are a well-made and well-looking race, but carry famine in their aspect. Are often a whole summer without a grain in the island; which they regret not on their own account, but for the sake of their poor babes. In the present economy of the island, there is no prospect of any improvement. . . .

A number of black cattle is sold, at thirty or forty shillings per head, to graziers, who come annually from Skie, and other places. The mutton here is small, but the most delicate in our dominions, if the goodness of our appetites did not pervert our judgment: the purchase of a fat sheep was four shillings and six pence: the natives kill a few, and also of cows, to salt for winter provisions. A few goats are kept here: abundance of mares, and a necessary number of stallions; for the colts are an article of commerce, but they never part with the fillies. . . .

Very few poultry are reared here, on account of the scarcity of grain.

(Pennant *A Tour in Scotland and
Voyage to the Hebrides*, 1772)

A full generation before the clearance in Rum, economic pressure was beginning to mount.

In Rum, there is a considerable number of small native sheep; their flesh is delicious, and their wool valuable. A quantity of it is sent yearly to the Redcastle market, near Inverness, where it often sells at 14s. the stone, while other wool sells about half that price. This island seems best calculated for rearing sheep, being almost wholly covered with hills and high mountains, but the proprietor's attachment to the inhabitants, has hitherto prevented its being stocked with *them only*.

(M'Lean *Old Statistical Account,
Parish of Small Isles*, 1794)

It is let in six farms, at the rent of about £500 a year.
Colonel M'Lean of Coll is the proprietor, who in 1801
insisted that one of the farms should be stocked with sheep.
The farmer with much reluctance complied with his
landlord's injunction, but instead of stocking his farm fully,
he only put one half of the number of sheep the farm would
feed; notwithstanding, he sold the wool of the half stock
of sheep the first year for £50 and the rent of the whole
farm was only £60.

(Murray *Companion and Useful Guide to the
Beauties of Scotland*, visit of 1802)

The islanders of Rum are reputed the happiest of the
Hebrideans; both on account of the low rent which Mr
Maclean receives for his farms, and because the isle
furnishes a great number of large and small cattle, which
supply them all with meat. Their principal occupations
are the care of cattle, fishing, and the gathering of sea-
weed, which they burn for the purpose of extracting alkali.

(Necker de Saussure
Voyage to the Hebrides, 1807)

Of course it couldn't last. The community occupation of
Rum was over within a few years. Virtually the entire
population was cleared in 1826 and 1828.

Muck and Eilean nan Each

THE HORSE IYLE. Be foure of sea toward the southeist,
layes ane little ile, half ane myle lang, callit be the Eriche
Ellannaneache, that is in Englishe the Horse ile, guid for
horse and uther store.

(Monro *A Description of the Western
Isles of Scotland*, 1549)

The sense is that the Irish (i.e. the Gaels) call the island
Eilean nan Each.

144

SWYNES ILE. Be ane haffe myle of sea to this ile, lyes ane ile of twa myle lang, callit in Erische Ellannaneche, that is the Swynes ile, and very fertill and fruitful of cornes and grassing for all store, and verey guid for fishing, inhabit and manurit.

(ibid.)

There is a mistake in this second extract since Eilean nan Each refers to Muck's subordinate isle which Monro has just described.

Next . . . there is ane Illand called Illand Muck that is to say the hoggisilland and it is on the southend of [Eigg]. It is verie profitabill and fertill of corne and abundance of milk and fish in this Illand.

(Mitchell (ed.) *Macfarlane's Geographical Collections*, p. 175, ?1590s)

It . . . is fruitful in corn and grass.

(Martin *A Description of the Western Islands of Scotland, c.* 1695)

This little island, however it be named, is of considerable value. It is two English miles long, and three quarters of a mile broad, and consequently contains only nine hundred and sixty English acres. It is chiefly arable. Half of this little dominion the laird retains in his own hand, and on the other half, live one hundred and sixty persons, who pay their rent by exported corn.

(Johnson *A Journey to the Western Islands of Scotland*, 1773)

It is very fertile in corn, of which they export some; and its coasts abound in fish.

(Boswell, *Journal of a Tour to the Hebrides*, 1773)

Muck . . . is mostly arable, and exports some barley, oats, potatoes, and cattle.

> (Knox *A Tour through the Highlands of*
> *Scotland and the Hebride Isles in 1786*)

There are no sheep in Isle Muck.

> (M'Lean *Old Statistical Account*, 1794)

Muck . . . is a low fertile island, well adapted for the rearing of black cattle, and for the cultivation of green and corn crops . . . The grass is of the finest description. Upon the whole, it is a beautiful little island.

> (Maclean *New Statistical Account,*
> *Parish of Small Isles*, 1836)

Beauty notwithstanding, Muck was partly cleared in 1828. Between 1821 and 1831 the population halved.

Eigg

EGGA . . . gude maine land . . . and verey guid for store, namelie for sheip.

> (Monro *A Description of the Western*
> *Isles of Scotland*, 1549)

Eigg seems to have held a good stock of sheep in St Donnan's day and in 1549. This may always have been a characteristic feature of Eigg's pastoral economy.

Eig. This Illand is profitable and fertill of corne and milk.

> (Mitchell (ed.) *Macfarlane's*
> *Geographical Collections*, p. 175, ?1590s)

Eg is ane Ile verie fertile and commodious baith for all kind of bestiall and corns, speciallie aittis, for eftir everie boll of aittis sawing in the same ony yeir will grow 10 or 12 bollis agane.

(Skene *The Description of the Isles of Scotland*, 1577–95)

It is all rocky and mountainous from the middle towards the west; the east side is plainer, and more arable: the whole is indifferent good for pasturage and cultivation.

(Martin *A Description of the Western
Islands of Scotland, c.* 1695)

Egg . . . is mountaneous and more fit for pasture than Corn . . . and their Chief Employment both here and in Canna, is to take Care of their Cattle.

(Bruce, Report in *Hardwicke Papers, c.* 1750)

It rises towards the West, into several Rocky Hills . . . but from these, it shelves towards the East, where there are many fine Fields both of Grass and Corn.

(Walker *Report on the Hebrides*, 1764)

Egg . . . is considerably larger than Muck, but not so fruitful.

(Knox *A Tour through the Highlands of
Scotland and the Hebride Isles in 1786*)

Of Eigg primarily:

The crop seldom affords the inhabitants a competent subsistence. For several years past, a considerable quantity of meal has been annually imported, it having been necessary to feed their cattle with a great part of their own crop, during the winter season, especially when severe. . . . Last year, 1793, the crop was not all got in till near the end of November. . . . One farm in Eigg was begun to be stocked with black faced sheep, about two years ago. They seem to multiply and thrive well.

(M'Lean *Old Statistical Account*, 1794)

When we look at a Highland landscape today we are often struck by the sheer desolation. This was not always the case; cultivation and manure increased the fertility of the soil so we should imagine it as formerly speckled with patches of green. Hugh Mackinnon describes Grulin after it had been cleared and put under sheep in the following year:

> There was not a ewe on the land of Grulin that did not have twins. The land was so rich and so fertile after being cultivated and well manured by the poor wretches who had gone to America: when the sheep stock was put on it there was not a ewe there that did not have twins. Yes. Yes: that's what I used to hear them saying.
>
> (Mackinnon *Tocher 10*, 1973)

Unfortunately two centuries of sheep-grazing have completely degraded much of the Highland landscape.

Agriculture remained the way of earning a living in the islands into the nineteenth century. It became an increasingly inadequate means of support but the fact that potatoes thrived in Highland conditions led to every scrap of available ground being cultivated.

> Agriculture, with the rearing of black-cattle and sheep, is the prevailing occupation in these islands. The sea-weed, both that which is cut, and that which is cast ashore by the winter storms, is the chief manure. With the aid of this, the people generally raise as many potatoes, (on which they for the most part subsist,) as are requisite for their maintenance during the whole of the year – each family requiring from 240 to 320 bushels. From 300 to 400 heads of black-cattle are annually sold in the parish to dealers at home, who again bring them to the south country markets for sale. The number of sheep pastured in the Island of Rum alone is about 8000, which are all of the black-faced kind, and which are likewise all salved or smeared.
>
> (Maclean *New Statistical Account*, 1836)

Despite the Revd Maclean's optimistic spin, the population of Eigg more than halved between 1841 and 1891.

Shielings and transhumance

The pastoral economy of the Highlands and Islands involved transhumance, or the transfer of stock to high pastures during the summer. This practice is also found in Norway and Highland place-names include those which begin with *Airidh* or *Ari-* (the Gaelic form for shieling) and those which end with *-ary* or *-ery* (the Norse form). Throughout the Hebrides, islanders took advantage of small islets in the same way. Eigg has Eilean Chathastail, Muck has Eilean nan Each. Their souming arrangements were carefully calculated.

> Every inhabited island has its appendant and subordinate islets. Muck, however small, has yet others smaller about it, one of which has only ground sufficient to afford pasture for three wethers.
>
> (Johnson *A Journey to the Western Islands of Scotland*, 1773)

> On the south coast of Eigg, there is a small island, called Eillan Chastel, which is good for pasture, and a pendicle of a contiguous farm in Eigg. A few persons, tending cattle, live upon it during a part of the summer months only. . . . On the north-west side of Isle Muck, lies Eillean nan Each, Island of Horses. . . . This island is of inconsiderable extent, but good for pasture.
>
> (M'Lean *Old Statistical Account*, 1794)

Miller gives us a picturesque account of a remote shieling midway down the east coast of Eigg. Although his account dates from 1845 the practice had been maintained for perhaps thousands of years, and was just about to collapse.

> Rarely have I seen a more interesting spot, or one that, from its utter loneliness, so impressed the imagination. The shieling, a rude low-roofed erection of turf and stone,

with a door in the centre some five feet in height or so, but with no window, rose on the grassy slope immediately in front of the vast continuous rampart. . . . Save the lonely shieling, not a human dwelling was in sight. An island girl of eighteen, more than merely good-looking, though much embrowned by the sun, had come to the door to see who the unwonted visitors might be . . . There was a turf fire at the one end, at which there sat two little girls, engaged in keeping up the blaze under a large pot, but sadly diverted from their work by our entrance; while the other end was occupied by a bed of dry straw, spread on the floor from wall to wall, and fenced off at the foot by a line of stones. The middle space was occupied by the utensils and produce of the dairy, – flat wooden vessels of milk, a butter-churn, and a tub half-filled with curd; while a few cheeses, soft from the press, lay on a shelf above. The little girls were but occasional visitors, who had come out of a juvenile frolic, to pass the night in the place; but I was informed . . . that the shieling had two other inmates, young women, . . . who were out at the milking, and that they lived here all alone for several months every year, when the pasturage was at its best, employed in making butter and cheese for their master

(Miller *The Cruise of the Betsey,* 1845)

Shielings were, of their nature, temporary structures – designed simply for use in the summer. On the mainland they seem to have been built of timber and turf and lasted only a few years. In Rum the scarcity of trees meant that shielings were built entirely of stone, using corbel techniques that had been used in the islands since the Early Christians constructed their beehive cells. There are some 400 ruined shielings in Rum which demonstrate intense, if not necessarily very ancient, occupation. Records suggest Rum was sparsely inhabited until about the mid-seventeenth century. Its population then exploded, quite possibly because people were brought in from other islands. Most of these shielings may date from the period 1650 to 1825.

Industry

There is no Species of Industry carried on, either in this, or the three adjacent Islands of Rum, Eig and Muck, so that the People are idle to the Last Degree. It would be happy for them, was there a Spinning School erected in Canna for the Use of the four Islands.

(Walker *Report on the Hebrides*, 1764)

Canna

All the clothing is manufactured at home: the women not only spin the wool, but weave the cloth: the men make their own shoes, tan the leather with the bark of willow, or the roots of the Tormentilla erecta, or tormentil, and in defect of wax-thread, use split thongs. . . .

Rum

For want of lime they dress their leather with calcined shells: and use the same method of tanning it as in Cannay.

(Pennant *A Tour in Scotland and Voyage to the Hebrides*, 1772)

Speaking of the Laird of Muck

Many trades they cannot have among them, but upon occasion, he fetches a smith from the Isle of Egg, and has a tailor from the main land, six times a year.

(Johnson *A Journey to the Western Islands of Scotland*, 1773)

Of the parish in general:

There are 8 male and 6 female weavers, 1 house-carpenter, and 5 boat-carpenters, 5 taylors, and 2 smiths. Most of these, besides their respective trades, spend a considerable part of their time in fishing, labouring, and other necessary occupations. There are few or no seamen, except those who follow the fishing during a part of the year. There are two merchants, who bring their goods from the Glasgow market. There is one clergyman of the Established church, one Roman Catholic priest, one surgeon, and one schoolmaster; all these have their residence in Eigg.

(M'Lean *Old Statistical Account*, 1794)

Among the inhabitants are some artisans, such as weavers, boat-builders, smiths, tailors, and one shoemaker: but although these devote some of their time to the various employments of their calling, yet they chiefly depend upon their agricultural occupations for their subsistence.

(Maclean *New Statistical Account*, 1836)

Shoemaking

Among the various things brought aboard this morning, there was a pair of island shoes for the minister's cabin use, that struck my fancy not a little. They were all around of a deep madder-red colour, soles, welts, and uppers; . . . were sewed not unskilfully with thongs; and their peculiar style of tie seemed of a kind suited to furnish with new idea a fashionable shoemaker of the metropolis. They were altogether the production of Eigg, from the skin out of which they had been cut, with the lime that had prepared it for the tan, and the root by which the tan had been furnished, down to the last on which they had been moulded, and the artizan that had cast them off, a pair of finished shoes. There are few trees, and, of course, no bark to spare, in the island; but the islanders find a substitute in the astringent lobiferous root of the Tormentilla erecta, which they dig out for the purpose among the heath, at no inconsiderable expense of time and trouble.

I was informed . . . that the infusion of root had to be thrice changed for every skin, and that it took a man nearly a day to gather roots enough for a single infusion. I was further informed that it was not unusual for the owner of a skin to give it to some neighbour to tan, and that, the process finished, it was divided equally between them, the time and trouble bestowed on it by the one being deemed equivalent to the property held in it by the other.

(Miller *The Cruise of the Betsey* 1845)

Milling in Rum

Notwithstanding this island has several streams, here is not a single mill; all the molinary operations are done at home: the corn is graddan'd, or burnt out of the ear, instead of being thrashed: this is performed two ways; first, by cutting off the ears, and drying them in a kiln, then setting fire to them on a floor, and picking out the grains, by this operation rendered as black as coal. The other method is more expeditious, for the whole sheaf is burnt, without the trouble of cutting off the ears: a most ruinous practice, as it destroys both thatch and manure, and on that account has been wisely prohibited in some of the islands. Graddaned corn was the parched corn of Holy Writ . . . The grinding was also performed by the same sort of machine the quern, in which two women were necessarily employed . . . I must observe too that the island lasses are as merry at their work of grinding the Graddan . . . as those of Greece were in the days of Aristophanes,

Who warbled as they ground their parched corn.

The quern or bra is made in some of the neighboring counties, in the mainland, and costs about fourteen shillings. This method of grinding is very tedious: for it employs two pairs of hands four hours to grind only a single bushel of corn. Instead of a hair sieve to sift the meal the inhabitants here have an ingenious substitute, a sheep's skin stretched round a hoop, and perforated with small holes made with a hot iron. They knead their bannock with water only, and bake or rather toast it, by laying it upright against a stone placed near the fire.

(Pennant *A Tour in Scotland and
Voyage to the Hebrides*, 1772)

Rural societies are notoriously conservative but few Highland communities could justify taking their corn to a central mill to be ground. It was much more economical to do it at home with a hand-quern. Like other repetitive tasks such as waulking or rowing the participants would sing in order to maintain a rhythm and relieve the tedium.

Trees

Timber was enormously important in the Highlands, as a building material as much as for fuel. Whatever woodland there was in the Small Isles was probably cut down as the population grew.

Rum, a wooded and hilly island.

(John of Fordun *Chronicle of the
Scottish Nation, c.* 1380)

Rum . . . the north end produces some wood.

(Martin *A Description of the Western
Islands of Scotland, c.*1695)

In all of the above Islands there is great plenty of Turff for fireing; but no kind of Timber.

(Bruce, Report in *Hardwicke Papers, c.* 1750)

Canna, at this time, is destitute even of a gooseberry-bush.

(Edward Daniel Clarke, 1797)

Plans for forestry in Rum were being mooted nearly 250 years ago:

> But as the Bulk of the Island is defended from the Strong South West Wind by a ridge of Mountains, it is likely that Wood would thrive well upon it; nor is it probable that it can ever be turned to so much account, as by being sown entirely with the Seeds of the various Timber, and Converted into a Forest. It has once been well wooded, and in some of the steep Gullies, inaccessable to Cattle, the Oack, the Birch, the Holly, and Rowan Tree, are still to be observed growing vigorously.

(Walker *Report on the Hebrides*, 1764)

Rum – of the trees by what was then Kinloch House:

> These trees were planted about fifty years ago; and their fine, healthy appearance, now, is strong evidence of what might be done in these bare, mountainous Hebridean isles by plantation. This compact clump of wood at Kinloch House looks very striking, seen from the bay; and it looks all the more so because the rest of the island is as bare of trees as a lapstone. With the exception of this bit of woodland, I don't believe there is another tree on the island bigger than the gooseberry trees in the garden at Kinloch House.

(Waugh *The Limping Pilgrim*, 1882)

Fuel

In the absence of woodland, the islanders were entirely dependent upon peat for fuel. It became a particular problem in Canna and Muck.

THE SMALL ISLES

Canna

Fuel is very scarce here, and often the inhabitants are obliged to fetch it from Rum.

(Pennant *A Tour in Scotland and Voyage to the Hebrides*, 1772)

Fuel – The fuel consists principally of peats, to which heath must be frequently added. In Eigg there is a competency of peats and heath; in Rum abundance; in Canna there is no heath for fuel, and their store of peats is not so abundant. Formerly Rum helped to supply Canna in peats, but of late years the island supplies itself, except a quantity of coal imported from the Clyde, by the principal tacksman, and some peats, he now carries from the coast of Sky, for the use of his family. Isle Muck, within itself, is ill provided in fuel. Formerly they were provided in peats by Rum and Ardnamurchan; of late their supplies were solely from Rum, with much personal toil and danger. From Eigg, they import boat loads of heath, when their peats become scarce. In winter 1790 and 1791, there was a general scarcity of firing throughout this parish, which Isle Muck most severely felt. They were reduced to the necessity of burning different kinds of furniture, such as beds, dressers, stools, barrels; and also house timber, divots, tangles, straw, etc. to dress their victuals. Bringing heath from Eigg was a constant employment when the weather permitted. . . . Indeed the people of Isle Muck get a great part of their fuel, and summer grass for their horses, in Rum, as a gratuity, during pleasure, from its proprietor to the proprietor of Isle Muck, who is a cadet of his family.

(M'Lean *Old Statistical Account*, 1794)

After the clearance in Rum they seem to have reverted to Ardnamurchan.

Muck

Here there is no peat for fuel, so that the people are under the necessity of importing this necessary article of household economy from the mainland of Ardnamurchan.

(Maclean *New Statistical Account*, 1836)

Rum

Little conical black piles, here and there, show the places where the inhabitants get peat for firing.

(Waugh *The Limping Pilgrim*, 1882)

Housing

In June 1700 Bishop Nicolson was visiting the isolated Catholics of the west coast. He was rowed from Arisaig to Eigg.

The houses of this, and indeed of all the other islands, are not constructed of wood, like those of the mainland (for in the Isles there is no wood except what is imported), but the walls are extremely thick. The two faces of the wall are of stone and the space between is filled in with earth in the manner of an embankment or rampart against the cold winds which blow from the ocean in winter.

(Blundell *Catholic Highlands of Scotland*, 1917)

Pennant found a similar situation in Rum:

At the bottom of the bay is the little village Kinloch, of about a dozen houses, built in a singular manner, with walls very thick and low, with the roofs of thatch reaching a little beyond the inner edge, so that they serve as benches for the lazy inhabitants, whom we found sitting on them in great numbers, expecting our landing, with that avidity for news common to the whole country.

Entered the house with the best aspect, but found it little superior in goodness to those of Ilay; this indeed had a chimney and windows, which distinguished it from the others, and denoted the superiority of the owner: the rest knew neither windows nor chimnies. A little hole on one side gave an exit to the smoke: the fire is made on the floor beneath; above hangs a rope, with the pot-hook at the end to hold the vessel that contains their hard fare, a little fish, milk, or potatoes.

(Pennant *A Tour in Scotland and*
Voyage to the Hebrides, 1772)

Airs . . .

Social sensibility is extraordinarily powerful. In the same way that people today eschew street numbers on their houses in favour of exotic or romantic names so the Laird of Muck fought a long battle to escape his title.

Among other guests, which the hospitality of Dunvegan brought to the table, a visit was paid by the laird and lady of a small island south of Sky, of which the proper name is Muack, which signifies swine. It is commonly called Muck, which the proprietor not liking, has endeavoured, without effect, to change to Monk. It is usual to call gentlemen in Scotland by the name of their possessions, as Raasay, Bernera, Loch Buy, a practice necessary in countries inhabited by clans, where all that live in the same territory have one name, and must be therefore discriminated by some addition. This gentleman, whose name, I think, is Maclean, should be regularly called Muck; but the appellation, which he thinks too coarse for his island, he would like still less for himself, and he is therefore addressed by the title of, Isle of Muck.

(Johnson *A Journey to the Western*
Islands of Scotland, 1773)

Saturday, 18 September, 1773

A young gentleman of the name of M'Lean, nephew to the Laird of the Isle of Muck, came this morning; and, just as we sat down to dinner, came the Laird of the Isle of Muck himself . . . It was somewhat droll to hear this laird called by his title. Muck would have sounded ill; so he was called Isle of Muck, which went off with great readiness. The name, as now written, is unseemly, but is not so bad in the original Erse, which is Mouach, signifying the Sows' Island. Buchanan calls it Insula Porcorum. It is so called from its form. Some call it Isle of Monk. The laird insists that this is the proper name. It was formerly church-land belonging to Icolmkill, and a hermit lived in it.

(Boswell *Journal of a Tour to the Hebrides*, 1773)

Of course 'Monk Island' was pure fiction. As a former possession of Iona the island of Muck may indeed have housed a hermit but this argument was presumably dredged up by the Laird of Muck to give a fig-leaf of rationality to his claim. Muck appears as 'Mok' in Fordun's list of islands dating from about 1380. It appears on Nowell's map of *c.* 1565 as Muk, and a spate of others thereafter. It was a straightforward Gaelic description and can be compared with other forms such as Glenmucklach in Kintyre. The island's shape is nothing like a pig and we can assume it received its name because it once housed pigs, in exactly the same way as Eilean nan Each once pastured horses.

The pretence nearly worked. In 1801 George Langlands called the island 'Monk Island' in his map of Argyllshire. Normally, getting one's name on the map is sufficient to guarantee immortality but happily Langlands lacked the force of the Ordnance Survey. Truth will out; Muck resurfaced and Muck it is likely to remain.

Johnson, whose tongue was as barbed as his nature, was nevertheless capable of the sharpest insights. He saw straight to the heart of the problem which was that the cultural conversion of the Highland chiefs spelled doom for their own people. Boswell reports his comment on the subject of their anglicisation:

> Sir, the Highland chiefs should not be allowed to go farther south than Aberdeen.
>
> (Boswell, *Journal of a Tour to the Hebrides*, 1773)

. . . and Graces

Poverty, curiosity and hospitality were three impressions formed by early visitors to the Small Isles. Pennant's description of the sorry houses at Kinloch in Rum was accompanied by this compliment:

> Yet, beneath the roof I entered, I found an address and politeness from the owner and his wife that were astonishing: such pretty apologies for the badness of the treat, the curds and milk that were offered; which were tendered to us with as much readiness and good will, as by any of old Homer's dames, celebrated by him in his Odyssey for their hospitality. I doubt much whether their cottages or their fare was much better; but it must be confessed that they might be a little more cleanly than our good hostess.
>
> (Pennant *A Tour in Scotland and Voyage to the Hebrides*, 1772)

The following story illustrates the customary deference to the chief's family as well as hospitality to visitors.

> We landed near a farm, called . . . Guaridil, and immediately several of the islanders came to welcome Mr Maclean,

the brother of their Laird. We accompanied him into the cottage of one of his brother's tenants . . .

Returning to Guaridil, we found the old man, who received us at landing, waiting, with his bonnet in his hand, to request that we would honour his cottage with a short visit. Mr M. conducted us in, when we were agreeably surprised to find a clean but homely cloth spread upon a board between two beds, which served us for chairs, upon which was placed a collation of cream, eggs, new-milk, cheese, oat-cakes, and several bottles of the fine old Lisbon wine we had before so much relished.

(Edward Daniel Clarke, 1797)

Today, people often mourn the loss of the impromptu entertainment, the ceilidh, the warmth of hospitality. MacCulloch gives an example of how vital this could be:

Again attempting Rum, we landed at Scuir More; but at the imminent risk of losing our boat among the breakers and rocks of this most impracticable shore. In half an hour it blew a hurricane, and all hopes of re-embarking vanished. With the assistance of the villagers of Guirdil, the boat was hauled up dry, and we made up our minds to remain a week; by no means an unlikely event. But we should not have been starved, while there was a Highlander who had a potatoe. We were in at least as much danger of being devoured with kindness. One hoped that if I visited his neighbour, I should also come to him. 'The house of one, was only two miles off; that of another, only five.' 'I could surely pass one night at Papadill; or one at Kilmorie;' 'it was but a bittie over the hill.' But as it was impossible to go to all, it ended, as was natural, in taking up with the nearest Maclean who spoke the best English. If I am to be wrecked any where, I will choose Rum . . .

in ten minutes the potatoe kettle was put on the fire, and my boat's crew was provided with such fare as the house afforded. I was taken into the parlour, and regaled

161

with tea; for, as in England of old, this is a precious article, and given as a treat at any time of the day. . . . But the day wore on, the potatoes were eaten, there was nothing to do, and it continued to blow and rain . . . The neighbours had come to see the strangers; and a considerable ogling began to take place among some of my handsome lads and the damsels. There was an old fiddle hanging up in a corner, very crazy in the pegs and in the intestines, but still practicable. . . . at length, by dint of the boatswain's mate, a little philosophy, and a little oakham, the pegs were repaired and the strings eked out, as well as if Straduarius himself had had the management of the business.

MacCulloch himself played the fiddle.

The musician gained great credit and applause: never probably having been half so much esteemed or admired in his life, in any society, before or since. . . . A ball here requires no great preparations, it must be allowed. The lasses had no shoes, and marvellous little petticoat; but to compensate for those deficiencies, they had abundance of activity and good-will. I suppose I ought to admire Highland dancing, fling and all; and if I do not, it is not for want of abundant experience. But the people are fond of it; they enter into it with heart and soul, as well as with all the limbs of their body, and it makes them very happy; and if all these are not good reasons in favour of any system of dancing, I wish some one would discover better. . . .

But all human happiness must end. . . . The sun blazed out beneath the cloud, and the fiddle ceased. But I protracted the evil hour as long as I could, in tender pity to the prettiest girl of the party, who had been sudden and quick in falling in love with a handsome lad belonging to my crew, and was weeping bitterly at the thoughts of parting. As the wind filled our little sail and swept us over the rolling sea, I saw the last wave of poor . . . [Peggy

Maclean's] hand, as she stood advanced on the point of a
rock, with her long hair streaming in the storm.

(MacCulloch *The Highlands and
Western Isles of Scotland*, 1824)

Beneath the rough exterior John MacCulloch was
obviously an old sentimentalist. His heart reached out to
the poor girl, desperate in the isolation of Rum. A
handsome sailor arrives and to Peggy Maclean her island
must have seemed a desolation, not the paradise we make
it today.

Reality or sentiment?

Like Janus, history faces two ways. Its substance is the
past, but its form is of the present. It is therefore laden
with our moral judgements, our hopes and aspirations for
the future. Highland history faces a particular predicament:
the past has been so damaging and the present so
precarious, that our judgements carry more weight than
they might elsewhere. Sentiment has disguised reality.

Retrospection is often clouded by emotion, and islands
are especially evocative. Whether it be St Kilda or the
Small Isles an astonishing amount of ink and energy has
been expended on their salvation. Over the years umpteen
schemes of improvement for the Highlands and Islands
have come and gone. As early as 1794 the minister, Donald
M'Lean, proposed something like a planned economy for
the Small Isles:

Eigg seems pretty equally divided as to crop and pasture
grounds, and, in plentiful seasons, should maintain its
present inhabitants. Canna, Isle Muck, and Rum, are not
inconveniently situated, mutually to assist each other, if a
plan proper for this purpose were adopted. Rum might

help the summer grazing of Canna and Isle Muck, and render their cattle fitter for market. Canna and Isle Muck might afford a surplus of crop to supply the inhabitants of Rum. In the former islands fuel is scarce; in the latter, moss is plentiful.

Admirable – but such ideas proved powerless against the larger economic process. The fundamental problem was that agriculture did not offer the islanders a sufficiently robust base – and they could not find an alternative.

Donald M'Lean's proposals point up a continuing dilemma for the Highlands and Islands. How accurate or misplaced are our judgements? Are they based on raw emotion, or historical reality? Are we correctly interpreting economic trends? Are we supporting the right ventures or are we just trying to hold back the tide? Are we being practical or self-indulgent? At the heart of a great deal of the debate about the future of the Highlands is a highly romanticised and sentimental view of the past. The economy of the Small Isles was always marginal: life could be sustained, but at a level we are no longer prepared to accept, not for ourselves and certainly not for our children. At our level of expectation the economic base can only support a fraction of the former population.

The weather is a good topic for summarising this dilemma. Good because we are all interested in it and better because it carries no moral burden. Is the weather improving or getting worse? Amidst our current concerns about climate change Donald M'Lean's comments in 1794 remain topical:

It is remarked by the inhabitants, that the seasons are still becoming more and more rainy. For a few years past, even the winters have been attended with rain, instead of the usual snow and frost.

Of course we all look back to the sun-drenched days of

youth. What is difficult to know is whether his observations were true, or simply nostalgic; fact or false memory? For many visitors the weather of Rum becomes particularly memorable. The last word had better go to the grizzled honesty of John MacCulloch:

> There is a great deal of stormy magnificence about the lofty cliffs, as there is generally all round the shores of Rum . . . The interior is one heap of rude mountains, scarcely possessing an acre of level land. It is the wildest and most repulsive of all the islands. The outlines of Halival and Haskeval are indeed elegant, and render the island a beautiful and striking object from the sea. . . . If it is not always bad weather in Rum, it cannot be good very often; since, on seven or eight occasions that I have passed it, there has been a storm, and on seven or eight more in which I have landed, it was never without the expectation of being turned into a cold fish. 'The bitter breathing winds with boist'rous blasts' seem to have set up their throne here, as at Loch Scavig: and the rains too. Like that place, it possesses a private winter of its own, even in what is here called summer.
>
> (MacCulloch *The Highlands and Western Isles of Scotland*, 1824)

7

Population and resources

DID IT HAVE TO end?
Before the days of the Welfare State, subsidies and
economic planning, the key to island prosperity was the
relationship between population and resources. This has
been the critical issue throughout the history of the
Small Isles. Although this problem became visible to
the outside world during the period 1750–1800 it may
have been endemic. What demographic statistics we
have suggest the population was always young and with
a slight majority of females. Such conditions threaten
population increase if natural checks and balances do
not obtain.

What were these checks and balances? – Starvation and
disease! We know nothing about either of these factors
before the eighteenth century but can suspect they were
effective. The received wisdom is that the population of
the Highlands and Islands began to explode between about
1750 and 1841. Perhaps it had always threatened to outrun
resources but had previously always been checked.

Tables 1–5 give some population statistics for the Small Isles. These include estimates made on the basis of levy figures dating from the end of the sixteenth century. We are also very fortunate that the Small Isles were chosen by John Walker as a demographic case-study for his report on the Hebrides.

> The four Islands of Eig, Rum, Muck and Canna, compose what is called the Parish of the Small Isles. I was anxious to obtain an accurate List of the People, in one of the Parishes of the Hebrides, and pitched upon this for the Purpose. I engaged with this View a sensible and careful Man, who is Catechist in the Parish, to make an Accurate Roll of the Inhabitants in the Course of his annual Visitation. To mark the Number of Families, and how many persons were contained in each; the Number of Marriages and of Children; and the Age of each individual in the Parish. The following Table and Observations, comprehend the Substance of his Report, which was very accurate and particular; and the Facts founded upon them, will be found applicable, I believe, with very little Variation, to all the other Parishes of the Western Islands.

(Walker *Report on the Hebrides*, 1764)

Walker notes that in Rum many children are servants in other families. Nineteenth-century census returns in mainland districts like North Morar confirm this. In a close-knit society it evened out the distribution of children and was dictated partly by economics, partly by a form of social service. Walker's figures have been analysed by Margaret Mackay in her book *The Rev Dr John Walker's Report on the Hebrides*.

The population figures for the Small Isles are very different from those of Britain today. An age pyramid would show a broad base and a narrow tip. Lots of children were born, many died young, few survived into what we would call old age. There was also an imbalance between

Table 1 Eigg

Year	Houses	Families	Males	Females	Total	Source	Density
c. 1595					(250/300)	Skene (60)*	
1625					198+	Giblin**	
1728					(390)	SPCK***	
1750					260	D.Bruce	
1755					345	Webster	
1764		88	183	276	459	Walker	5.22
1768					501	OSA	
1794					399	OSA****	
1801	87	87	217	283	500	Census	5.75
1807					400	de Saussure	
1811	75	75	201	241	442	Census	5.89
1821	87	87	224	245	469	Census	5.39
1831	74	74	215	237	452	Census	6.11
1841					546	Haswell-Smith	
1891					233	Haswell-Smith	
1931					138	Haswell-Smith	
1991					69	Haswell-Smith	

* No of fighting men supplied by Skene's anonymous report (1577–95). The range for total population is between 250 (on the basis of Walker's ratio) and 300 (using Webster's ratio).
** The Franciscan missionary Cornelius Ward converted 198 in Eigg. This did not include at least one family who were related to the minister.
*** SPCK figure of 340 over the age of 5 given by J. L. Campbell. Using Walker's table of ages from 1764 we can project that total population would be about 390.
**** Donald M'Lean, minister, wrote in the *Old Statistical Account* that 176 people had left Eigg in 1788 and 1790. Fortunately we have the passenger lists for three vessels which sailed from Arisaig to North America in July and August 1790. Seven people from Eigg went on the *Jane*, 21 on the *Lucy* and 32, all from Cleadale, on the *British Queen*.

Table 2   Rum

Year	Houses	Families	Males	Females	Total	Source	Density
c.1595					(30/35)	Skene (6/7)*	
1625					17+	Giblin**	
1728					(179)	SPCK***	
1755					206	Webster	
1764		57	147	157	304	Walker****	5.33
1768					302	OSA	
1772		59			325	Pennant	5.51
1773		58				Johnson	
1786					300	Knox	
1794					443	OSA	
1807					443	de Saussure	
1821	65	65	177	217	394	Census	6.06
1831	15	15	73	61	134	Census	8.93
1841					124	Haswell-Smith	
1891					53	Haswell-Smith	
1991					26	Haswell-Smith	

* No of fighting men supplied by Skene's anonymous report (1577–95). The range for total population is between 30 (on the basis of Walker's ratio) and 35 (using Webster's ratio).
** The Franciscan missionary Cornelius Ward only converted 17 in Rum (in contrast to 198 in Eigg). Ward also noted that there were only three villages in Rum.
*** SPCK figure of 152 over the age of 5 given by J. L. Campbell. Using Walker's table of ages from 1764 we can project that total population would be about 179.
**** Walker commented that many of the young had left the country or were servants in other families. In 1764 Rum had the highest proportion of young children in the Small Isles. Population grew fast between 1600 and 1764 which suggests a change of policy. As Maclean ownership became more firmly established it was probably abandoned as a game reserve and stocked with Maclean adherents who multiplied frequently.

Table 3 Canna

Year	Houses	Families	Males	Females	Total	Source	Density
c. 1595					(84/100)	Skene (20)*	
1728					(253)	SPCK**	
1750					210	D. Bruce	
1755					231	Webster	
1764		44	124	129	253	Walker	5.75
1768					233	OSA	
1772					220	Pennant	
1794					304	OSA	
1807					300	de Saussure	
1821	73	73	206	230	436	Census	5.97
1831	45	45	124	140	264	Census	5.87
1841	44		116	139	255	J. L. Campbell	5.80
1851	45		125	113	238	J. L. Campbell	5.29
1861	29		55	72	127	J. L. Campbell	4.38
1891	21		53	49	102	J. L. Campbell	4.86
1931	14		31	29	60	J. L. Campbell	4.29
1991					20	Haswell-Smith	

* No of fighting men supplied by Skene's anonymous report (1577–95). The range for total population is between 84 (on the basis of Walker's ratio) and 100 (using Webster's ratio).

** SPCK figure of 236 over the age of 5 given by J. L. Campbell. Using Walker's table of ages from 1764 we can project that total population would be about 253.

Table 4 Muck

Year	Houses	Families	Males	Females	Total	Source	Density
c.1595					(72/80)	Skene (16)*	
1728					(140)	SPCK**	
1755					161	Webster	
1764		28	72	71	143	Walker	5.11
1768					172	OSA	
1773					162+	Johnson	
1773					142+	Boswell	
1786					253	Knox	
1794					193	OSA***	
1821	57	57	145	176	321	Census	
1831	25	25	70	85	155	Census	5.63
1841					68	Haswell-Smith	6.2
1891					48	Haswell-Smith	
1991					24	Haswell-Smith	

* No of fighting men supplied by Skene's anonymous report (1577–95). The range for total population is between 72 (on the basis of Walker's ratio) and 80 (using Webster's ratio).

** SPCK figure of 128 over the age of 5 given by J. L. Campbell. Using Walker's table of ages from 1764 we can project that total population would be about 140.

*** We know from Donald M'Lean, the minister, that a number of people left the island in 1788 and 1790.

171

THE SMALL ISLES

Table 5 Small Isles

Year	Houses	Families	Males	Females	Total	Source	Density
c. 1595					(436/515)	Skene (102/103)*	
1652					800/900	J. L. Campbell** ***	
1728					(962)		
1755					943	Webster	
1768					1208	OSA	
1794	252		648	691	1339	OSA****	
1811	279	279	711	836	1547	Murray	5.31
1821	282	282	752	868	1620	Census	5.54
1831	159	159	482	523	1005	Census	5.74
1841					993	Murray	6.32
1881					541	Murray	
1991					139	Haswell-Smith	

* No of fighting men supplied by Skene's anonymous report (1577–95). The range for total population is between 436 (on the basis of Walker's ratio) and 515 (using Webster's ratio).

** 800 or 900 were converted in Eigg, Rum(?) and Canna, according to Father Dugan.

*** Sum of island projections.

**** Donald M'Lean, writing for the *Old Statistical Account*, states that 238 emigrated from the Small Isles in 1788 and 1790.

Webster reckoned the number of fighting men at one-fifth of the total population.

Walker's ratio is taken from the actual numbers of Fencible Men (16–60 years old) he found in the Small Isles. Expressed as a proportion of the whole this ratio was a little higher than Webster's.

males and females. More males were born, and died, leaving females making up a slight majority of the population. Pennant noticed this at the time and even added a footnote comparing the situation in the Small Isles to Chester.

> Rum . . . is the property of Mr Macleane, of Col; a landlord mentioned by the natives with much affection. . . . the number of souls at this time three hundred and twenty-five; of families only fifty-nine . . . They had with them a hundred and two sons and only seventy-six daughters: this disproportion prevails in Cannay, and the other little islands; in order, in the end, to preserve a ballance between the two sexes; as the men are, from their way of life, so perpetually exposed to danger in these stormy seas, and to other accidents that might occasion a depopulation, was it not so providentially ordered.*
>
> * In Chester, and other large towns, tho' the number of males exceeds the number of females born; yet when arrived to the age of puberty the females are much more numerous than males; because the latter, in every period of life, are more liable to fatal diseases.
>
> (Pennant *A Tour in Scotland and Voyage to the Hebrides*, 1772)

Disease

Rum

> The Island was then accounted populous, as it had not been visited by the Small Pox for 29 years; for by this Disease upon former Occasions, it had been almost depopulate. There were 125 People, 24 of them married Persons who had never had the Small Pox, and who then lived in the greatest Dread, as the Disease had lately appeared in some of the Adjacent Islands.
>
> (Walker *Report on the Hebrides*, 1764)

The inhabitants of Rum are people that scarcely know sickness: if they are attacked with a dysentery they make use of a decoction of the roots of the Tormentilla erecta in milk. The small-pox has visited them but once in thirty-four years, only two sickened, and both recovered. The measles come often.

(Pennant *A Tour in Scotland and Voyage to the Hebrides,* 1772)

Canna

Sickness seldom visits this place: if any disorder seizes them the patients do no more than drink whey, and lie still. The small-pox visits them about once in twenty years.

(Pennant *A Tour in Scotland and Voyage to the Hebrides,* 1772)

Johnson and Boswell give an example of old-fashioned paternalism at work in Muck:

The laird having all his people under his immediate view, seems to be very attentive to their happiness. The devastation of the small-pox, when it visits places where it comes seldom, is well known. He has disarmed it of its terrour at Muack, by inoculating eighty of his people. The expence was two shillings and sixpence a head.

(Johnson *A Journey to the Western Islands of Scotland,* 1773)

Last year he had eighty persons inoculated, mostly children, but some of them eighteen years of age. He agreed with the surgeon to come and do it, at half a crown a head.

(Boswell *Journal of a Tour to the Hebrides,* 1773)

Infant mortality was high:

The diseases, which most commonly appear in this parish,

174

are the continued fever, croup, erysipelas, measles, catarrh, pleurisy, epilepsy, hooping cough, diarrhoea, dropsy of the belly, and jaundice. Of these the most fatal are the croup, pleurisy, and hooping cough. About two years ago, the croup proved very mortal, and swept away many children, some of them about 9 or 10 years of age.

(M'Lean *Old Statistical Account*, 1794)

Relationship of population to resources

Contemporary observers noticed the high level of population relative to the quantity of land.

Rum

The Island contains 288 Inhabitants, and 53 Acres for each Person. The Number of Families in it are 52, that is above 5 persons to each Family. . . . Such a Number of People, living in the way of Husbandry, upon so small a Property is not perhaps to be found anywhere else in Europe.

(Walker *Report on the Hebrides*, 1764)

Muck

The proportion of the people to the land is such, as the most fertile countries do not commonly maintain.

(Johnson *A Journey to the Western Islands of Scotland*, 1773)

One cause of this was the subdivision of land to each new generation. In 1794 the minister, Donald M'Lean, wrote of the reasons for the heavy emigration from the Small Isles in 1788 and 1790.

A principal cause of this emigration was, that the country was overstocked with people, arising from frequent early

> marriages; of course, the lands were able to supply them but scantily with the necessaries of life. It is not unfrequent, upon these occasions, for a parent to divide with his newly married son, the pittance of land (sometimes a very small portion of a farm) possessed by him, which must reduce both to poverty and misery.

If subdivision was part of the problem then so was landlord pressure. In the very next sentence M'Lean writes:

> Another cause of the emigration is, that the island of Eigg, which was formerly in part rented by small tenants, was divided among 8 principal tacksmen.

We have seen how sheep made economic sense in Rum long before the island was cleared. Some landlords put sentiment above rents but this proved a temporary respite. In the long run sheep were more profitable than people.

Two resources were seized upon as offering future prosperity – kelp and fishing. It was not just in the Small Isles. They were the focus of attention throughout the Highlands and Islands. Despite all the effort and invest-ment the fishing industry never took off in the west as it did on the east coast of Scotland. The riches of the sea were not enjoyed by Highlanders, a problem that has still not been fully addressed. The kelp industry brought enormous wealth to a very few people for a short space of time, and then it collapsed.

Fishing

Muck

SWYNES ILE. . . . verey guid for fishing.

> (Monro *A Description of the Western Isles of Scotland*, 1549)

Its coasts abound in fish.

> (Boswell *Journal of a
> Tour to the Hebrides*, 1773)

Eigg

Eig . . . abundance of fish in the sea about that Illand but they have no skill to slay the said fish.

> (Mitchell (ed.) *Macfarlane's Geographical
> Collections*, pp. 175–6, ?1590s)

Canna

KANNAY . . . guid for . . . fishing.

> (Monro, *A Description of the Western
> Isles of Scotland*, 1549)

Cainna . . . with abundance of all kynd of seafishes.

> (Mitchell (ed.) *Macfarlane's Geographical
> Collections*, p. 177, ?1590s)

The south end hath plenty of cod and ling.

> (Martin *A Description of the Western
> Islands of Scotland, c.* 1695)

There are several Cod Banks within reach of the Island, but the Inhabitants never fish but to supply themselves.

> (Walker *Report on the Hebrides*, 1764)

The people of Canna fish a good deal with the long line, and both catch and cure ling.

> (Wilson *Voyage Round the Coasts of
> Scotland*, vol. I, 1842)

The principal kinds of fish caught upon these coasts are herrings, cod, and ling. The herrings are some years caught in Loch Scresort in Rum, during the month of August; but the inhabitants being ill provided in fishing materials, seldom catch a competency for their own families. The cod and ling are caught mostly on the coasts of Canna and Isle Muck, the fishing ground being most convenient to the harbours in these islands. They are exported to the Clyde market, and the ling sold from £3 to £3 10s per 120 ling. The Cearban or sun-fish [basking-shark] appear in May, and sometimes remain till July. Their liver alone is useful for making oil some of them yielding 12 barrels. This oil is also most frequently exported to the Clyde market. Different other kinds of fishes are caught, of some benefit to the inhabitants.

(M'Lean *Old Statistical Account*, 1794)

The sail fish, or . . . basking shark . . . generally lie motionless, on the surface of the water, as if asleep, . . . A hot sunshine day is the best time to prosecute this fishery with success. . . . The liver is the only useful part, and yields, particularly in the female, from six to eight barrels of pure sweet oil, very proper for lamps, and much valued by tanners, who buy it at £3 per barrel.

(Knox *A Tour through the Highlands of Scotland and the Hebride Isles in 1786*)

The problem with fishing was that boats and gear were needed if it was to be done on any scale. The islanders did not have the resources, even of the most basic things. When Pennant visited Canna he found that:

Fish and milk was their whole subsistence at this time: the first was a precarious relief, for, besides the uncertainty of success, to add to their distress, their stock of fish-hooks was almost exhausted: and to ours, that it was not in our power to supply them. The rubbans, and other trifles I had brought would have been insults to people in distress. I lamented that my money had been so uselessly laid out;

for a few dozens of fish-hooks, or a few pecks of meal, would have made them happy.

(Pennant *A Tour in Scotland and Voyage to the Hebrides*, 1772)

Pennant saw clearly that one of the handicaps that the Highlanders faced was the high capital investment required. The industry had to be turned from an adjunct of household economy into a commercial business. He found out for himself that it was beyond the reach of almost all Highlanders.

Abundance of cod and ling might be taken; there being a fine sand-bank between this isle and the rock Heisker, and another between Skie and Barra; but the poverty of the inhabitants will not enable them to attempt a fishery. When at Campbeltown I enquired about the apparatus requisite, and found that a vessel of twenty tuns was necessary, which would cost two hundred pounds; that the crew should be composed of eight hands, whose monthly expences would be fourteen pounds; that six hundred fathom of long-line, five hundred hooks, and two Stuoy lines (each eighty fathoms long) which are placed at each end of the long-lines with buoys at top to mark the place when sunk, would all together cost five guineas; and the vessel must be provided with four sets: so that the whole charge of such an adventure is very considerable, and past the ability of these poor people.

(Pennant *A Tour in Scotland and Voyage to the Hebrides*, 1772)

In such circumstances the landowner required to be a venture capitalist. Few were suited to the task. John Knox came up the west coast to prospect for possible fishing stations on behalf of the British Fisheries Society. He sailed through a thick fog to Loch Scresort in Rum.

Here we landed, at a small village, in a situation not unpleasant. The people were all busy in packing herrings for their winter provision; and more might have been cured, if they had been provided with salt. Mr Maclean, the proprietor of Coll, informed me, that he was determined to give the inhabitants of that island every assistance for promoting the fisheries. I hope he will extend his benevolent endeavours to this bay also, by erecting a small key [quay], and supplying the people with salt and casks, for which they would pay ready money. By means of this aid, they would furnish all the inhabitants of the island in herrings, or white fish, through the whole year.

(Knox *A Tour through the Highlands of Scotland and the Hebride Isles in 1786*)

Knox saw that one obstacle to the development of the fishing industry was the difficulty of obtaining cheap salt for curing. We have local confirmation of this:

The salt laws are an object of great complaint in this parish, as well as in its neighbourhood. The late alterations in these laws have facilitated the getting, at a moderate rate, salt for curing fish; but still the custom-house forms, to which every purchaser of such salt must submit, may be considered as a real grievance. If a person wishes to procure 2 or 3 barrels of such salt, to cure fish for the use of his family, he must enter it in a custom-house, if it should be 50 miles distant; he must grant bond and security for it. The fish salted therewith, he must proceed with to a custom-house, however distant; there he must unship and repack it, and all this trouble and expence for a few barrels for his own family use. . . . The lower class, who are the bulk of the people, are often at a loss for this necessary article of life, from the severity of the present salt laws. They will have it on the easiest terms possible, whatever be the means; and the difficulty of obtaining it in a fair, encourages an illicit trade.

(M'Lean *Old Statistical Account*, 1794)

180

Edward Daniel Clarke reinforced this view. Mr Maclean, his informant, was brother of the Laird of Coll and was visiting Rum with Clarke.

A slight alteration in the excise laws, respecting the article of salt, would produce a very rapid change in favour of the Highlanders. For want of this necessary article, some hundreds of them, during the present year, will be compelled to manure their lands with the fish they have taken; if they were permitted to manufacture it themselves, all Europe might be supplied from these islands, with the fish they would be enabled to cure. But, as the law now stands, the natives are constantly in perplexity and distress. If salt is to be had, the regulations respecting it are so complicated, that none of them understand them; by which means they are continually involving themselves in lawsuits and difficulties. Add to this, the great distance to which they are obliged to go, in order to procure the salt; the expense attending which, together with the trouble, and the danger of trusting their crazy boats to the uncertainty of the seas, discourages them from attempting to cure their fish, and checks the progress of industry. The nearest custom-house to the island of Rum is Tobermorey. When they arrive there, they are under the necessity of entering into a bond with regard to the salt they purchase, and make oath, under heavy penalties, that every grain of salt they take home, is to be altogether and entirely appropriated to the curing of fish. When the operation of curing the fish is completed, if a single gallon of the salt remains, they must make another voyage to the custom-house, with the salt and the fish they have cured; display both before the officers of the customs, and take up their bond. But if any part of the salt thus purchased is found afterward in their houses, they become immediately subject to penalties, sufficiently burdensome to ruin them entirely, or effectually to put a stop to their future industry. If the year prove unfavourable, and a scarcity of salt prevail, as is the case at present, they are not only deprived of the means of pursuing their fishing to advantage, but even deprived of sustenance for their families during the winter; although Providence has blessed their shores with every necessary, even to abundance, and the power of preserving the plenty thus bestowed is constantly within their view.

(Edward Daniel Clarke, 1797)

Of course to sustain a fishing industry the boats needed a good harbour for landing in.

Harbours

Muck

SWYNES ILE . . . with ane guid heighland haven in it, the entrey quherof is at the west cheik.

(Monro *A Description of the Western Isles of Scotland*, 1549)

There is no safe harbour in it, but small boats are secured by means of a quay, built by the inhabitants.

(Maclean *New Statistical Account*, 1836)

Rum

The bay Loch-Scresord on the east side is not fit for anchoring, except without the entry.

(Martin *A Description of the Western Islands of Scotland, c.*1695)

This harbour is only open to the eastward, and consequently there is seldom any great swell. It is spacious, its ground good, its depth of water from 5 to 7 fathoms, and is a good outlet either north or south . . . This harbour, to be frequented, needs only to be better known, as it is not only commodious in itself, but lies convenient for supplies of beef and mutton at a very moderate rate.

(M'Lean *Old Statistical Account*, 1794)

Eigg

With a haven for heighland bottis.

(Monro *A Description of the Western Isles of Scotland*, 1549)

There is a harbour on the south-east side of this isle which may be entered into by either side the small isle without it.

(Martin *A Description of the Western Islands of Scotland, c.* 1695)

Traditional Highland boats were galleys or birlinns: clinker-built vessels, descended from Viking models, which could be sailed or rowed as conditions offered. They were the military and commercial vehicles of the West Highlands for about 900 years and the linchpin of the area's economy. After about 1603 they went into terminal decline and replacements tended to come from outside the Highland area.

In mediaeval times, as the above extracts show, Highland birlinns were versatile enough to land in all sorts of unlikely places. Later fishing boats depended on sail alone and needed a safe haven in bad weather. Canna was always regarded as the best harbour in the Small Isles. As Knox said of the others:

In these islands there are some anchoring places, but no good harbours.

(Knox *A Tour through the Highlands of Scotland and the Hebride Isles in 1786*)

Canna

> And when scutts boats or gallys cannot land in Cainna
> nor in Haysgair nor yet in Tiry The ancient Inhabitants
> and principall of these Countries do say that saids Gallies
> boats nor scutts can nowayes land neither in Scotland
> England nor yet in Ireland.
>
> (Mitchell (ed.) *Macfarlane's Geographical
> Collections*, p. 177, ?1590s)

Great hope was held out for Canna harbour on the grounds
that it was a haven for passing traders.

> ISLE CANNAY
> There is good anchorage on the north-east of this isle.
>
> (Martin *A Description of the Western
> Islands of Scotland, c.* 1695)

> Canna . . . is capable of great Improvement being Centrical
> to most of the Western Islands On the East side of which,
> there is a large Commodious and safe Harbour where most
> Ships from Ireland and the West Coasts of England, and
> Scotland touch at, in their way to and from the Baltique.
>
> (Bruce, Report in *Hardwicke Papers, c.* 1750)

> Canna is a very pleasant and fertile small Island with a
> fine Harbour: much frequented by the Ships which pass
> through the Hebrides.
>
> (Walker *Report on the Hebrides,* 1764)

The reason for Knox's journey in 1786 was to ascertain
the best fishing stations for possible investment by the
British Society for Extending the Fisheries. He wanted to
visit:

> Canay, the only small island in the Hebrides that has any
> claim to a village on the plan, and out of the fund of the
> British Society . . . It lies . . . directly in the track of shipping

184

to and from the Baltic. It is surrounded by fishing banks, and having a harbour sufficient to contain ships of burden, such vessels as cannot make the harbours of the Long Island on one side, or Tobirmory on the other, generally run for Canay.

(Knox *A Tour through the Highlands of Scotland and the Hebride Isles in 1786*)

Canna accordingly appears in Knox's list of proposed 'stations for villages' in the Hebrides. Unfortunately, despite protracted negotiations, nothing came of it.

The harbour of Canna is the most beautiful in all the Hebrides. It is small, but safe and commodious.

(Edward Daniel Clarke, 1797)

Here is an excellent harbour; well sheltered, safe and commodious. In former times, it was much frequented, particularly by the Baltic traders, and is still frequented by shipping of every description.

(Maclean *New Statistical Account*, 1836)

Sadly, Canna harbour did not take off. With the advent of steam there was less need for safe havens, and boats became less dependent on wind and tide. One more economic opportunity fell aside.

Some observers compared west coast fishermen to those from the east coast – to the former's disadvantage. But in truth they were not comparable, for the former never had the money to invest in boats and gear. Even without, they drew compliments.

It may be questioned if there are anywhere else on the West Coast such daring and successful small-boat sailors as are found in Muck.

(Robertson 'Topography and Traditions of Eigg', 1898)

However, in common with fishermen elsewhere they were very superstitious. There was a curious sea-taboo at work whereby the islanders were not allowed to refer to their islands by name when at sea.

Canna

The natives call this isle by the name Tarsin at sea.

Eigg

The natives dare not call this isle by its ordinary name of Egg when they are at sea, but island Nim-Ban-More, i.e., the isle of big women.

(Martin *A Description of the Western Islands of Scotland, c.* 1695)

Tradition says, that of old the islands forming this parish, had names sometimes given them different from those which they now bear: Thus Eigg was called Eillan nan Banmore, (the Island of the Great Women); Rum was called Rioghachd na Forraiste Fiadhaich, (the Kingdom of the Wild Forrest); Canna was called An t-eillan tarssuin, (the Island lying across); and Isle Muck, Tirr Chrainne, (the Sow's Island). But these may be supposed poetical names, given by the Gaelic bards; and the superstitious are said to have used them, and them only, when at sea, and bound for these islands.

(M'Lean *Old Statistical Account*, 1794)

The Revd Robertson explains the logic behind this:

The intention of the use of those alternative names by the superstitious when at sea and bound for those islands was probably to conceal the destination from witches and other malign powers, which, with the illogic of superstition, were supposed to know the islands only by their true name.

(Robertson 'Topography and
Traditions of Eigg', 1898)

Kelp

Kelp is seaweed whose ash was used in the manufacture of soap and glass.

Canna

About twenty tuns of kelp are made in the shores every third year.

(Pennant *A Tour in Scotland and
Voyage to the Hebrides*, 1772)

The kelp was cut every second or third year.

The expence of cutting down, drying, and burning, is generally £1 11s 6d per ton; and the price in Scotland is from £4 to £5.

(Knox *A Tour through the Highlands of
Scotland and the Hebride Isles in 1786*)

On this basis the landowner made a clear profit of over £2 per ton. In the context of the Long Island, Knox was informed that in 1784 Clanranald's estate had produced 900 tons of kelp. Prices rose dramatically during the Napoleonic Wars.

The inhabitants of Canna, like those of the neighbouring islands, are chiefly occupied in the manufacture of kelp. Cattle and kelp constitute, in fact, the chief objects of commerce in the Hebrides. The first toast usually given on all festive occasions is – 'a high price to kelp and cattle'.

In this, every islander is interested, and it is always drunk with evident symptoms of sincerity. The discovery of manufacturing kelp has effected a great change among the people; whether for their advantage or not, is a question not yet decided. I was informed in Canna, that if kelp keeps its present price, Mr Macdonald, of Clanranald, will make £6,000 sterling by his kelp.

But the neglect of tillage, which is universally experienced since this discovery was made, is already sensibly felt . . . The lands lie neglected, and without manure . . . The great scarcity of barilla, arising from the war with Spain, has considerably augmented the speculations of all the Western islanders, with regard to their kelp, which is expected to bear a very high price.

The manufacture of kelp is conducted by the following process:

The sea-weed is first collected and dried. The usual mode is to cut a portion of kelp annually from the rocks, taking it from the same place only once in three years. After the kelp has been dried, it is placed in a kiln prepared for the purpose, of stones loosely piled together, and burned. After it is consumed, and the fire is to be extinguished, a long pole pointed with iron is plunged into it, and it is stirred about; the result of the burning being, by this time, a thick glutinous liquid, which runs from the kelp in burning. As soon as this liquid cools, it hardens, and the operation is at an end. It is then shipped off to market. The usual expense of manufacturing kelp, is about two guineas a ton for the labour; if it is sold on the shore, which is generally the case, and estimating the kelp only at eight guineas a ton, the proprietor clears six.

(Edward Daniel Clarke, 1797)

Unfortunately the kelp industry did not last. There is plenty of evidence that, for a short period of time around the Napoleonic Wars, the industry fared spectacularly well in the Hebrides. Such was the nature of economic power, and the ownership of resources, that this wealth was not evenly distributed. As John Knox pointed out in 1786 the proprietors spent the wealth of the Highlands elsewhere:

> As the value of its natural produce, by sea and land, is almost wholly absorbed by the great landholders, and by many of them spent at Edinburgh, London, Bath, and elsewhere; as the people are thus left more or less at the mercy of stewards and tacksmen, the natural resources of the country, instead of a benefit, become a serious misfortune to many improveable districts.

Kelp became a great missed opportunity.

The problem was that there were only limited sources of wealth. We have seen how hunting and gathering continued to be an essential part of the economy of the Small Isles until recently. Apart from what they could gather the only other resources available were what they could grow on land or fish from the sea. Land was a finite resource, and as population grew so did the disjunction between supply and demand. Potatoes provided a temporary solution in that they thrived in Highland soils and became the staple for most Highlanders from about 1750. However potatoes could not solve the larger economic problems, they could only relieve hunger.

There are not many ways out of this vicious economic circle. People have to die or leave, productivity has to increase, or new resources have to be found. At the end of the day productivity did not increase sufficiently, new resources did not last or could not be taken advantage of, population levels rose and people left.

Argument has always raged over whether they had to. Of course the Clearances involved dreadful injustice and the motives of landowners seldom bear examination. But even without clearance the economic fundamentals were stacked ever higher against small island communities. If we are to make comparisons then perhaps the situation in the Small Isles should be compared to the agonies of St Kilda rather than the brutalities of Sutherland or Knoydart.

Clearance and emigration

In 1788 and 1790 a total of 238 people left the Small Isles, 176 of them from Eigg. Most went to America. Rum was cleared of its population in 1826 and 1828. Muck was cleared of half its people in 1828. Community life ended abruptly in Rum, more slowly in the other islands.

Mrs Murray writes very cogently on the causes of emigration and in her own, characteristically sensible, way poses the dilemma that still bedevils us:

> It has been said, Government should interfere in order to prevent the Highland emigration. In this free country can Government interfere? Can it dictate to a proprietor of land to dispose of his property in any given mode? Or can it say to a free born people, you shall not leave the Highlands?
>
> (Murray *Companion and Useful Guide to the Beauties of Scotland*, 1803)

But at the same time Hugh Miller's epitaph remains relevant:

> It did not seem as if the depopulation of Rum had tended much to any one's advantage. The single sheep-farmer who had occupied the holdings of so many had been unfortunate in his speculations, and had left the island: the proprietor, his landlord, seemed to have been as little fortunate as the tenant, for the island itself was in the market; and a report went current at the time that it was on the eve of being purchased by some wealthy Englishman, who purposed converting it into a deer-forest. How strange a cycle! Uninhabited originally save by wild

animals, it became at an early period a home of men, who, as the gray wall on the hill-side testified, derived, in part at least, their sustenance from the chase. They broke in from the waste the furrowed patches on the slopes of the valleys, – they reared herds of cattle and flocks of sheep, – their number increased to nearly five hundred souls, . . . Then came the change of system so general in the Highlands; and the island lost all its original inhabitants, on a wool and mutton speculation, . . . And now yet another change was on the eve of ensuing, and the island was to return to its original state, as a home of wild animals, where a few hunters from the mainland might enjoy the chase for a month or two every twelvemonth, but which could form no permanent place of human abode. Once more, a strange and surely most melancholy cycle!

(Miller *The Cruise of the Betsey* 1845)

8

Opportunity and Expectation

CONTINUITY OF SETTLEMENT IS not just about resources. Adequate resources may be a necessary condition, but they are not necessarily sufficient. One of the threats to the continuing settlement of the Small Isles has simply been the rising expectations of the inhabitants. Until the eighteenth century few islanders knew much of the outside world. They certainly would not have thought themselves free to migrate to it. Their world was circumscribed by family, chief and clan; by tenantry and obligation; by linguistic, social and cultural pressure. Horizons were restricted, they might stretch to another island in the Hebrides, the mainland perhaps, but little further.

From the eighteenth century this horizon was exploded. America beckoned, the cities offered new opportunity, the promise of wealth. These changes affected the whole Highland area, but particularly the islands. Small islands cannot sustain much diversity. They could not support tradesmen or artisans, certainly not towns, markets and shops. From the end of the eighteenth century it was not just the economic life of the islands that was under threat. It was also their claim on the minds and loyalty of their inhabitants.

Freedom of choice has undone the islands quite as surely as the enormous economic changes of the last two centuries. Few were prepared to sacrifice the prospect of prosperity abroad for a narrow drudgery at home. Amidst all the raw emotion bandied about in the clearance controversy this simple issue is often overlooked. Why? Because we can assign no blame. We cannot blame the young for choosing to abandon the ways of centuries. Cultural loss is a tragedy, and in the face of tragedy we need a scapegoat. Landlords can certainly be blamed for clearance, but that is not the complete story. There is still the issue of voluntary emigration.

We can see some of these tensions at work in the Small Isles. From the eighteenth century, increased contact meant that local people could compare their lot with circumstances that obtained elsewhere.

In this parish, a spirit of discontent seems much to prevail. Many complain of their rents, and many of their want of schools, besides other inconveniences already suggested. . . .

In the course of the last 20 years, the dress in this parish, as well as the neighbourhood, both of men and women, has undergone a very considerable change. The men in general wear hats, short jackets, and long trowsers; instead of bonnets, short coats, and philabegs; and instead of the tartan short hose, stockings are pretty much used. The kerchief, formerly worn by married women, and the tonnac, or short plaid, worn by females in general, are now almost wholly out of use. Instead of these, caps of various fashions, short and long cloaks, great coats, and ribbands, have been substituted. The men, such of them especially as follow the fishing, find the change in their dress highly convenient, and it may be presumed that they borrowed it from the seafaring people, who frequented these isles. Some people think that it was introduced by the Highlanders, who served in the last American war. The change in the dress of the women may be thus accounted for: Most of our young women go to the low country for some weeks in harvest; this time they spend in shearing; and with the money thus earned they endeavour to dress themselves after the low country fashion; the fashion, thus introduced, raises an emulation among the women in general, and, of course, merchants are encouraged to import like articles. The periodical migration of our young women to the low country in harvest, is entirely with a view to dress. They seldom bring home any share of the price of their labour in cash, and they are a mean of encouraging an extravagance of dress. So intent are they on this object, that from Whitsunday to Martinmas, they will not accept of service at home; and, except the few weeks spent in the low country, they are a burden to their friends for this half year. If manufactures, particularly the woollen, were established among us, our young women might find constant employment at home, mutually advantageous to themselves and to the public.

(M'Lean *Old Statistical Account*, 1794)

We must take into account that this was written by a minister. He may have been a traditionalist, unsympathetic to the fripperies of fashion and the women who followed it; he may have been harsh in his condemnation. Nevertheless the Highland world was under attack whenever it came into contact with Lowland culture. Whatever may be said about the effects of the post-Jacobite Disclothing Act, persecution usually promotes defiance. In the case of the Small Isles it seems that Highland dress was abandoned by the men for convenience and by the women for choice.

194

The minister highlighted the dilemma faced by migrant workers then and since. How much of their earnings do they repatriate and how much do they spend on themselves? In the same way an older generation will always regard a younger generation as spendthrift and incapable of enduring hardship. This is a favourite theme of early Scots historians – that, formerly, men throve on harder and less frequent fare. We meet this in Rum:

> The only Articles exported from the Island, are some Black Cattle and Horses. As for Corn, there is no more of it raised, than what serves the People for Bread a few Months in Winter. During all the Summer, they live entirely upon animal Food, and yet are healthy and long lived. The year before I was there, a man had died in the Island aged 103, who was 50 years of Age before he had ever tasted Bread; and during all the Remainder of his long Life, had never eat of it from March to October, nor any other Food, during that part of the year, but Fish and Milk; which is still the Case with all the Inhabitants of the Island. I was even told, that this old man used frequently to remind the younger People, of the simple and hardy Fare of former Times, used to upbraid them with their Indulgence in the Article of Bread, and judged it unmanly in them to toil like Slaves with their Spades, for the Production of such an unnecessary Piece of Luxury.

> (Walker *Report on the Hebrides*, 1764)

But once they have seen more, most will not content themselves with less. From the nineteenth century, hunger was not the determinant it used to be. Hugh Miller noticed that the young men of Eigg no longer risked their lives in climbing for shearwaters.

> In former times . . . the people of Eigg, taught by their necessities, were bold cragsmen. But men do not peril life and limb for the mere sake of a meal, save when they cannot

help it; and the introduction of the potatoe has done much to put out the practice of climbing for the bird, except among a few young lads, who find excitement enough in the work to pursue it for its own sake, as an amusement.

(Miller *The Cruise of the Betsey*, 1845)

People left the island on a seasonal basis in order to find work elsewhere. Island life was long sustained by earnings in the Lowlands, but there was little surplus:

The cottars in Eigg contrive barely enough to earn at the harvest in the Lowlands, money sufficient to clear with their landlord at rent-day.

(ibid.)

When looking back at fragile island communities we tend to indulge in an orgy of sentiment. To exorcise this I finish with some reminders that this was a world with aspects we would not want to return to.

Education

For most islanders education was an expensive luxury until the end of the nineteenth century. Today it is a necessity. Since it is not economical to provide anything beyond primary education in a small island this takes the children away once they start their secondary school career. Realistically we cannot have it otherwise but educational opportunities elsewhere will always challenge the continuity of small and remote communities.

The eagerness of the people for education is very remarkable.

(Waugh *The Limping Pilgrim*, 1882)

Waugh tells a pitiful story of a shepherd's wife from Guirdil who came to Kinloch one day in search of accommodation for her son so that he could go to school for a while. She was unsuccessful but her endeavours made a deep impression on Waugh:

> Her husband was only a poor shepherd; and they had nine children, the youngest of which were twins. She could read and write a little, herself; and she had taught all her children the alphabet, – at least, all those who were of a teachable age. She had even taught one of her little girls to write a letter, – after a fashion. She had taught her to write it so that they could manage to understand it well enough, amongst themselves, – but she didn't think that any English body would be able to make it out. She was very sorry to see her children growing up and learning nothing; and in a place where there was no chance of their learning anything; and, now, the twins and the house together, took up so much of her time that she had no time to teach them as she used to do. Indeed, what could she teach them; for she knew very little herself. She told me all this as she sat in the kitchen at Kinloch House; and, when she had done talking, she gave a deep sigh, and looked quietly around, as if she didn't know where on earth to turn for help; and I can only say that I felt downright sorry for that poor soul as she went back homeward up the wild mountain side that night.

(Waugh *The Limping Pilgrim*, 1882)

This story would pull at anyone's heartstrings, although it could be repeated countless times through rural Britain in the nineteenth century. We will always look back for a golden age, and in the context of the Small Isles it usually basks in a sort of warm Celtic glow where people somehow led fuller, more rounded lives. But would we want to return to this?

Waugh goes on to tell of one youth from Papadil, Kenneth Chisholm, who did have accommodation at Kinloch.

197

The lad is about fourteen years of age; he looks as hardy and as shaggy as a highland colt, and he can hardly understand you if he is addressed in English; but, like all the rest, he seems quite eager to learn. He comes nine miles over a wild mountain track every Monday morning, and sometimes in very rough weather; he gets his porridge and milk, two or three times a day, in the kitchen, here; and he sleeps at night with Kenneth Maclean's children at 'Carn-an-Dorian'; and he goes whistling back over the hills to his father's solitary homestead, every Saturday morning, as content as a king; carrying with him into that secluded spot all the news of the busy world upon the shore of Scresort Bay.

(ibid.)

Where would you meet this today? Not in the developed world, not in a country where we have grown accustomed to the concept of universal free education, where we have turned it into a right. Perhaps in a developing country, where people have no such luxuries, where education is seen as a means to escape and improve oneself. We are but five generations from Kenneth Chisholm, yet take for granted what he could only dream of. The irony of course is that nothing has killed the Gaelic language more swiftly and effectively than the Scottish education system.

Poverty

On our return to the *Betsey*, we passed through a straggling group of cottages on the hill-side, one of which, the most dilapidated and smallest of the number, the minister entered, to visit a poor old woman, who had been bed-ridden for ten years. Scarce ever before had I seen so miserable a hovel. . . . The walls and roof, formed of damp grass-grown turf, with a few layers of unconnected stone in the basement tiers, seemed to constitute one continuous hillock, sloping upwards from foundation to ridge . . . save where the fabric here and there bellied outwards or inwards, in perilous dilapidation, that seemed but awaiting the first breeze. The low chinky door opened direct into the one wretched apartment of the hovel, which we found lighted chiefly by holes in the roof. . . . Within a foot of the bed-ridden woman's head there was a hole in the turf-wall, which was, we saw, usually stuffed with a bundle of rags, but which lay open as we entered, and which furnished a downward peep of sea and shore, and the rocky Eilan Chasteil, . . . The little hole in the wall had formed the poor creature's only communication with the face of the external world for ten weary years. . . . I learned that not during the ten years in which she had been bed-ridden had she received a single farthing from the proprietor, nor, indeed, had any of the poor of the island, and that the parish had no session-funds. I saw her husband a few days after, – an old worn-out man, with famine written legibly in his hollow cheek and eye, and on the shrivelled frame, that seemed lost in his tattered dress; and he reiterated the same sad story. They had no means of living, he said, save through the charity of their poor neighbours, who had so little to spare; for the parish or the proprietor had never given them anything. He had once, he added, two fine boys, both sailors, who had helped them; but the one had perished in a storm off the Mull of Cantyre, and the other had died of fever when on a West India voyage; and though their poor girl was very dutiful, and staid in their crazy hut to take care of them in their helpless old age, what other could she do in a place like Eigg than just share with them their sufferings?

(Miller *The Cruise of the Betsey*, 1845)

Their daughter's devotion was admirable. But would any of us want this for our children today? Or would any young girl be content with the remoteness and desolation of the shieling Hugh Miller described?

9

From Support to Dependency

THROUGH ALL THEIR PREVIOUS history the Small Isles had functioned as self-sufficient units. They were not dependent upon support from outside. In bad years some people undoubtedly starved while the rest subsisted as best they could on the fruits of the sea-shore. Communities survived because they were young and hardy, and expectations were low. They lived on grain and farm animals, shellfish, sea-birds and fish. If a small population harvested such resources carefully they could survive from year to year. They could even render their owner some grain, butter and cheese, or livestock, hides and feathers. Their families maintained the chief and his retinue as they travelled round the estate while their menfolk supported his political and military ambitions when called upon. If times were particularly bad their chief might lay on a *creach*, or raid, in which some islanders would participate and hopefully bring home some spoil. It was, in a very rough and ready sort of way, an island equilibrium between resources and lifestyle.

So what happened? Why did it begin to fail? It was probably not because resources were over-used. With the exception of shellfish on certain beaches, the deer in Rum, and wood generally, the islanders probably did not exhaust their available resources. What happened was that the outside world changed, and then enforced change throughout the peripheries of Britain. The Industrial Revolution, urbanisation, economic growth elsewhere, offered lifestyles and longevity unheard of in the islands. Division of labour brought unquestionable efficiencies. Islanders were expected to match the productivity of Lowland Scotland and their resources simply didn't allow it. In the same way that productivity and the survival of communities are inextricably linked today, so they were then. Landlords were no longer content to receive a tiny money rent, a stone of butter or a quart of cheese and so many days military service. Owners did not want goats' hair or birds' feathers, they wanted cash. Money was the new medium, and everything had to be reckoned in these terms.

The old island economies could not cope with these modern requirements and, depending upon the speed with which their owners forced through change, they collapsed. The islanders looked for new means of earning a living and found some temporary success in kelp, or fishing, or soldiering during the Napoleonic Wars. But none of these created permanent industries and in the end every islander came to depend on his or her proprietor for work. Instead of the island economy maintaining a principal family or two, now the owner was expected to sustain the islander. Unless he or she was a very shrewd business person, or very rich, they simply could not manage. So, from the nineteenth century to the present every island has changed hands several times, each new owner trying to make a small and distant community, with few natural resources, economically viable. Some beneficent owners spent large amounts of money on islands they loved. In the end the level of investment and commitment required has seen through most of them. Now, Canna is owned by the National Trust for Scotland, Rum by Scottish Natural Heritage, Eigg is community-owned while Muck is still run as a small family estate.

These days there is a lot of talk about sustainable development, ethical investment, a desire to temper the excesses of capitalism. There is greater understanding of its insatiable appetite, its ruthless exploitation of every reserve to the point of exhaustion. Deforestation, sheep and fishing offer three particularly acute examples of the devastation caused by unrestricted capitalist development in a Highland environment. We have become more aware of its ability to destroy resource in one location whilst it creates wealth in another, its sacrifice of a countryside for the city. In abstract terms it matters not whether it is an impoverished Highland, or denuded Amazonian soil.

But there is another devil that has been unleashed by the triumph of capitalism and individualism, and that is expectation. Within the framework of western democracy the individual is king. He, or she, may agree to some partial diminution of their rights in the interests of social welfare or the common good. But generally our aspirations for personal wealth and satisfaction are neither checked nor questioned. Our appetites grow. We want more: a longer life, better health, more material goods. Our entire economic life is geared to satisfying this burgeoning demand. Adults sometimes try to escape, get away from it all, opt out: but our children are also fed the incessant advertisements of plenty.

This rise in expectations can only be met by ever-increasing productivity. And it is in this respect that the

Small Isles were, and will always be found wanting. A small island, with an economy based on agriculture and fishing, even with the seasonal boost of tourism, can never sustain the level of productivity required for a modern lifestyle. People who live there must do so from choice, or because they are subsidised, or have other incomes, or have to some extent opted out. All these reasons are sufficient for individuals; it remains to be seen whether they are sufficient for communities.

Ownership

At the beginning of the nineteenth century Clanranald was the dominant force in the Small Isles. He owned Eigg and Canna and had recently taken on Muck. Yet in 1827 he was constrained to sell his estates and since then the islands have each gone their own way under a succession of different owners. These changes are outlined below. Although the overall pattern is similar, the details vary from island to island. For those who wish to follow the process in individual islands I give the appropriate references.

Canna

The Macneill family, long-standing tenants on Canna, bought the island from Clanranald in 1827. The population, which had been 436 in 1821, fell to 127 in 1861. The Macneills sold it to the Thom family in 1881, who in turn sold it to J. L. Campbell in 1938, by which time the population had fallen to thirty-eight. In 1981 J. L. Campbell gifted Canna to the National Trust for Scotland who are its present owners. J. L. Campbell has given a comprehensive recent history in his book *Canna – The Story of a Hebridean Island*. Campbell was an eminent

Gaelic scholar and there is a long-term project for a Centre of Advanced Studies on the island.

Muck

Muck passed to the Macleans of Coll in the first quarter of the seventeenth century. It remained in this family until 1854, being temporarily held by Clanranald, who had taken on the Maclean debts, from 1799–1814. The population dropped from 321 in 1821 to 155 in 1831, primarily because of clearance. By 1841 the population had halved again. In 1854 Muck was sold to Captain Swinburne RN, a far-sighted man who experimented widely in the fishing industry and gave evidence thereon to the Napier Commission in Arisaig in 1883. He spoke presciently of the possibilities of fish-farming and the dangers of over-fishing. In 1896 Muck was purchased by Lawrence Thompson MacEwen who also bought Eigg. It has remained within this family since. Further details can be found in L. MacEwen's *The Island of Muck*.

Rum

Rum may have been acquired by the Macleans of Coll as early as the mid-fifteenth century although their ownership was not effective until the mid-seventeenth century. The population exploded between about 1650 and 1820. This may partly be because of natural increase, partly because it was stocked with tenants from elsewhere. In 1826 and 1828 Rum was completely cleared. In 1845 Maclean of Coll sold Rum to the Marquis of Salisbury and the island reverted to its former role as a retreat where an élite could pursue wildlife. This has been Rum's primary function for most of the last 700 years and continues today.

In 1870 Rum was sold to a family of Campbells and in 1888 it was bought by John Bullough whose son, George, built Kinloch Castle. What followed was a tale of opulence and extravagance, display and folly, grandeur and delusion. A magnificent castle was built with stone imported from Arran, surrounded by a garden laid with soil imported from Ayrshire. Now, in less than a century, there is a once-magnificent building sorely in need of attention, gardens rank with weeds and a pervasive sense of damp and decay as nature resumes her kingdom.

The story, a fairytale almost, is told by Noel Banks in *Six Inner Hebrides*, and Magnus Magnusson in *Rum: Nature's Island*. This way of life belonged to another age and, in the twentieth century, it fell apart under the pressure of economic and social change. In 1957 the Bullough family sold the whole of Rum (except the Mausoleum at Harris) to what was then the Nature Conservancy, now Scottish Natural Heritage. This, like other wildlife organisations, faces something of a credibility gap on the question of whether the island will continue to have a *human* history. As M. Nicholson, a former Director-General of the Nature Conservancy, said in 1994:

> We must have a larger tract of totally separate land, on which visiting and living would be strictly controlled so as to minimise every kind of human impact not essential to research and conservation.

> (Magnusson *Rum: Nature's Island*, 1997)

Rum is heavily subsidised.

Eigg

Eigg is the only one of the Small Isles whose ownership remained unchanged from early mediaeval times until the nineteenth century. It was part of the Macruari patrimony which passed down to the Clanranald branch of Clan Donald. In 1827 it was sold by Clanranald to Hugh Macpherson, an academic at Aberdeen University. His son Norman was to investigate the antiquities of the island later in the century. His interest in history notwithstanding, the population, which had been 546 in 1841, had fallen to 233 by 1891. In 1896 Eigg was sold, as was Muck, to Robert Lawrence Thompson MacEwen. In 1916 it was sold on to Sir William Petersen, a shipowner, and in 1926 to Sir Walter Runciman, father of Steven, the distinguished historian of the Crusades. By 1931 the population had fallen to 138. Historians are perhaps better at charting economic progress than making it.

In 1966 the Runcimans sold Eigg to Captain Robert Evans who sold it in 1971 to Bernard Farnham-Smith of the Anglyn Trust. He in turn sold it in 1975 to Keith Schellenberg and in 1995 Schellenberg sold the island to M. Eckhart. The last few years had been unhappy ones for the residents of Eigg but in 1997 they finally managed to secure the island in a community buy-out, most of the money for which came from an anonymous donor. This recent history is fully described by Camille Dressler in her book *Eigg – The Story of an Island*. At the time this process generated a great deal of political steam as it became bound up with the wider issue of land reform. Economic regeneration is another matter.

Ownership has always been important in a small island. Canna and Muck seem to have been owned by the church from the seventh century until after the Reformation. Rum was owned by a powerful family who maintained it almost as a royal game reserve. The later ownership of Canna and Eigg by Clanranald entangled them in the Jacobite Risings. But, with the possible exception of Rum, this variety of owners made little difference to the general economic and cultural background. The proprietors merely collected the fruits of their tenants' labours. These were paid largely in kind, or in service, or in entertainment. They were not paid in cash.

By about 1800 things had changed radically. Owners now wanted money rents which meant that their tenants had to buy and sell in the market-place. They were at a crucial disadvantage. They were far from the markets and dependent upon boats. They were being left out of a developing communications network based on land transport. If their products did not command a good price they could not pay the rent. From now on different landlords merely presided over an economy that was unravelling. As a result their own position became economically ever more important. When munificent owners spent generously, then an estate could survive. If they did not, it was simply not possible to earn a living and people left.

The population figures in Tables 1–5 tell the rest of the story. In each island the communities have dwindled. But there is a common economic and cultural history until about 1800: this is what we read about in the old accounts; this is what we see buried in the landscape; this is what I have tried to describe. Sometimes, as in the relationship with wildlife, it remains topical. Sometimes, as with the simplicity and rigour of the Early Christians, it continues to challenge thought and custom. The abstinence, the asceticism, of these early religious communities is still held up as an ideal. Every generation faces the same dilemmas, the same tension between selfish and altruistic impulse, between material and psychological satisfaction.

Expectation is a continuum along which we all take our place, deciding on an individual, family or community basis, how much we want or need by way of resources,

material goods, health care and education. Such decisions
are morally informed to the extent that we also make
judgements as to what is reasonable, and what is greed or
luxury. If we cannot generate these resources ourselves
then we must draw them from elsewhere in our region,
nation or superstate, and argue and compete with others
for them. We cannot, however, expect others to agree or
acquiesce in our choices if they have to fund them, or that
our children will be content with less once they have the
prospect of more.

Select Bibliography

Throughout this book I have followed the convention of referring to the 'Old' and 'New' Statistical Accounts. Technically the former was not 'Old'.

For Revd John Walker see under McKay.
For Edward Daniel Clarke see under Revd W. Otter.
For Boswell see under Johnson.

General

A. O. Anderson, *Early Sources of Scottish History*, vols 1–2, Stamford, 1990.

N. Banks, *Six Inner Hebrides*, Newton Abbot, 1977.

J. Bannerman, Notes on the Scottish Entries in the Early Irish Annals in *Studies in the History of Dalriada*, Edinburgh, 1974.

O. Blundell, *Catholic Highlands of Scotland (Western Highlands and Islands)*, 1917.

G. Broderick, *Chronicles of the Kings of Man and the Isles*, Manx Museum, 1979.

D. Bruce, Rentals for Eigg and Canna, E 744/1 in the National Archives of Scotland.

Calendar of Scottish Supplications to Rome 1423–28, Scottish History Society, 1956.

A. Cameron, *Reliquiae Celticae*, vol. 2, Inverness, 1894.

J. L. Campbell, *A Very Civil People*, Edinburgh, 2000.

T. O. Clancy and G. Markus (eds), *Iona – The Earliest Poetry of a Celtic Monastery*, Edinburgh, 1995.

Collectanea de Rebus Albanicis, Edinburgh, 1847.

G. Donaldson, *Scottish Historical Documents*, Edinburgh, 1970.

C. Giblin (ed.), *Irish Franciscan Mission to Scotland 1619–1646*, Dublin, 1964.

J. M. Gilbert, *Hunting and Hunting Reserves in Medieval Scotland*, Edinburgh, 1979.

Hardwicke Papers, Vol XCIX, British Library, Add MS 35447.

H. Haswell-Smith, *Scottish Islands*, Edinburgh, 1999.

I. Henderson, 'North Pictland, Appendix A' in *The Dark Ages in the Highlands*, Inverness Field Club, Inverness, 1972.

C. Hicks, *Animals in Early Medieval Art*, Edinburgh, 1993.

S. Johnson, & J. Boswell, *A Journey to the Western Islands of Scotland* and *The Journal of a Tour to the Hebrides*, Harmondsworth, 1984.

J. Knox, *A Tour through the Highlands of Scotland ... in 1786*, London, 1787.

R. G. Lamb, Coastal Settlements of the North, *Scottish Archaeological Forum* 5, Edinburgh, 1973.

The Life of Archibald McDonald of Barisdale, By an Impartial Hand, Edinburgh, 1754.

A. Macdonald, Two Major Early Monasteries of Scottish Dalriata: Lismore and Eigg, *Scottish Archaeological Forum* 5, Edinburgh, 1973.

M. M. McKay (ed.), *The Rev Dr John Walker's Report on the Hebrides of 1764 and 1771*, Edinburgh, 1980.

Revd Donald M'Lean, Parish of the Small Isles, 1794, in *The Statistical Account of Scotland*, Edinburgh, 1791–1799.

Revd Donald Maclean, Parish of the Small Isles, 1836, in *The New Statistical Account of Scotland*, Vol XIV, Edinburgh, 1845.

J. R. N. Macphail, ed., *Highland Papers*, vol IV, Scottish History Society, Edinburgh, 1934.

G. Markus, *Early Irish Feminism*, *New Blackfriars* 73, 1992.

M. Martin, *A Description of the Western Islands of Scotland c. 1695* (republished Edinburgh, 1994).

Miscellanea Scotica, vol 1, Glasgow, 1818.

A. Mitchell (ed.), *Macfarlane's Geographical Collections*, vol. II, Edinburgh, 1907.

Dean Monro, *A Description of the Western Isles, 1549* (republished Edinburgh, 1994).

T. S. Muir, *Ecclesiological Notes on some of the Islands of Scotland*, Edinburgh, 1885.

The Hon. Mrs Murray, *Companion and Useful Guide to the Beauties of Scotland,* 3rd edn, London, 1810.

L. A. Necker de Saussure, *Voyage to the Hebrides*, London, 1822 (written in 1807).

H. Palsson, & P. Edwards (trs.), *Eyrbyggja Saga*, Edinburgh, 1973.

H. Paton (ed.), *The Lyon in Mourning*, Edinburgh, 1895.

T. Pennant, *A Tour in Scotland and Voyage to the Hebrides 1772* (republished Edinburgh, 1998).

R. Pitcairn, *Ancient Criminal Trials in Scotland*, Edinburgh, 1883.

W. Reeves (ed.), *Life of St Columba*, Dyfed, 1988.

J. S. Richardson, *The Mediaeval Stone Carver in Scotland*, Edinburgh, 1964.

J. Robertson, *General View of the Agriculture in the County of Perth*, Perth, 1799.

N. Ross, *Heroic Poetry from the Book of the Dean of Lismore*, Scottish Gaelic Texts Society, 1939.

W.F. Skene, (ed.), John of Fordun's *Chronicle of the Scottish Nation*, vol 1, Reprinted, Llanerch Publishers, 1993.

W.F. Skene, The Description of the Isles of Scotland in *Celtic Scotland*, vol 3, Appendix III, Edinburgh, 1886–90.

W.J. Watson, Aoibhinn an obair an t-sealg in *The Celtic Review*, IX, 1913.

J. Wilson, *A Voyage round the Coasts of Scotland and the Isles*, vol. I, Edinburgh, 1842.

Rum

A. Cameron, *Bare Feet and Tackety Boots*, Luath Press, 1988.

T. H. Clutton-Brock and M. E. Ball (eds) *Rhum – The Natural History of an Island*, Edinburgh, 1987.

J. A. Love, *The Isle of Rum*, 1983.

J. MacCulloch, *The Highlands and Western Isles of Scotland*, vol. IV, London, 1824.

M. Magnusson, *Rum: Nature's Island*, Edinburgh, 1997.

P. Morgan, *Rum: Island Place-Names*, Scottish Natural Heritage, 1999.

Revd W. Otter, *The Life and Remains of Edward Daniel Clarke*, 2nd edn, 1825.

Rum: Kinloch Castle, Scottish Natural Heritage, 1999.

Rum: Nature's Island, Scottish Natural Heritage, 1999.

Edwin Waugh, *The Limping Pilgrim*, 1882.

C. R. Wickham-Jones, *Rhum – Mesolithic and later sites at Kinloch*, Edinburgh, 1990.

Eigg

O. Blundell, *Proceedings of the Scottish Antiquarian Society*, 47, 1913.

C. Dressler, *Eigg – The Story of an Island*, Edinburgh, 1998.

H. Mackinnon, *Tocher 10*, Edinburgh, 1973.

N. Macpherson, Notes on Antiquities from the Island of Eigg, *Proceedings of the Scottish Antiquarian Society* XII, 1876–8.

D. McDonald, Eigg and the '45, *Clan Donald Magazine* no. 13, Edinburgh, 1995.

H. Miller, *The Cruise of the Betsey*, Edinburgh, 1897 (written in 1845).

Revd C.M. Robertson, Topography and Traditions of Eigg, in *Transactions of the Gaelic Society of Inverness* vol. XXII, 1897–8.

J. Urquhart, *Eigg*, Edinburgh, 1987.

S. Wade Martins, *Eigg – An Island Landscape*, Countryside Publishing, 1987.

Canna

J. L. Campbell, *Canna – The Story of a Hebridean Island*, Oxford, 1984.

Royal Commission on the Ancient and Historical Monuments of Scotland, *Canna*, Edinburgh, 1999.

Muck

L. MacEwen, *The Island of Muck*, 1995.